Josephine Hannan

Told in the Gloaming

Or, our Novena, and how we made it

Josephine Hannan

Told in the Gloaming
Or, our Novena, and how we made it

ISBN/EAN: 9783337385651

Printed in Europe, USA, Canada, Australia, Japan

Cover: Foto ©ninafisch / pixelio.de

More available books at **www.hansebooks.com**

TOLD IN THE GLOAMING

OR

Our Novena, and how we made it.

BY

JOSEPHINE HANNAN

AUTHOR OF
"Leo," "From Darkness to Light," "Angels' Whispers and Angels' Kisses," "Sister Agatha."

Dublin
M. H. GILL AND SON
50 UPPER SACKVILLE STREET.
1884

TO

"AUNTIE,"

THIS LITTLE EFFORT

Is Dedicated,

WITH

AFFECTION TOO DEEP FOR WORDS,

WITH

GRATITUDE TOO HEARTFELT FOR EXPRESSION

BY

HER GOD-CHILD,

JOSEPHINE.

PREFACE.

THE child who was *réglementaire* in the Convent had just rung the big bell, warning the mistresses upstairs that the classes were over, when two little bodies jumped quickly off their stools in the large study-hall, and the little feet of their owners came twinkle, twinkle down the long room to where the mistress of the study stood.

"May we go?" said Veronica, the younger of them.

The mistress nodded assent, and then joining hands, the wee bodies left the room.

"She's not coming, I'm sure," said Helen, trying to pierce the darkness of the dim corridor.

"Let's wait a bit," insisted Veronica; "she's sure to come; she never misses, unless we've been naughty."

"Then let us go to the end of the corridor, and be there to meet her;" and so they went, hand-in-hand, to the glass door which separated the school part from the chapel precincts. Presently I heard a heavy footstep, and then a loud knock at my door, as I sat sewing beside the cosy fire in my little bedroom in the Lodge. I had hardly said "Come in," when a dear old French Sister entered and said: "Comment, vous abandonnez vos enfants; les voilà là bas, qui vous attendent !"

"Mais je croyais, ma sœur, qu'elles étaient sorties pour la journée," said I.

"Mais elles sont de retour," replied Sœur Cécile.

"Eh bien, je viens," I said; and folding up my work I went down to the glass door. "What, chicks," I said, "I thought you had gone out to spend the afternoon with Aunt Sophie?"

"So we did," said Helen; "but mamma was so upset, and so ill, and so tired, that we had to come back before tea."

Having left school, I was spending some time with my Mothers in the Convent, and they had given me this little mission to fulfil, namely, of taking these two little ones during the long morning and evening studies and trying to amuse them.

"Do you know," I began, when we were fairly seated in St. Joseph's, "that the Novena for the Feast of the Immaculate Conception begins to-morrow?—well, now, I've thought of a grand way for us three to keep it. Every evening, when I come to you, we will first kneel down and say our Novena, and then I will tell you a nice story. Won't that be nice?"

"Yes, yes," they cried together; "that will be nine stories!"

"Yes, nine stories," I said; "but there's one condition I must make, and that is that you will not once interrupt me while I am telling them, because they are just long enough for half an hour; and if the bell rang and surprised us you would have to go without hearing the end: and our practice shall be charity to everyone, shan't it?"

Both Helen and Veronica agreed to this condition; and the thought struck me, after the Feast of the Immaculate Conception was passed, "Might not some other little children besides Helen and Veronica like to hear the stories I told them, and to make, perhaps, next year the same Novena as we did?" And so, putting this thought into practice, I have written them, and I hope they will please you, dear little friends!

CONTENTS.

	PAGE
Dedication	v
Preface	vii
Novena	xv

FIRST NIGHT.

The Angelus Bell	3

SECOND NIGHT.

Short Legends and Anecdotes:

A Legend of Normandy	27
Faith	29
Mater Admirabilis	41

THIRD NIGHT.

The Gift the Christ-Child brought	49

FOURTH NIGHT.

Miss Swippie	75

FIFTH NIGHT.

The Loss of the "Hesperus"	99
The Rescue of the "Armistice"	110

SIXTH NIGHT.

Up the Tamar in a Steam-boat, and down a Tin-mine in a Basket	123

Contents.

	PAGE
SEVENTH NIGHT.	
Voices from the West	153
EIGHTH NIGHT.	
A Ten Miles' Gallop, and what came of it	187
Katie's First Communion	195
NINTH NIGHT.	
Anecdotes:	
A Legend	206
An Adventure on Lough Swilly	215
Barcelona	222

NOVENA

PREPARATORY TO

The Feast of the Immaculate Conception.

For ever praised and adored be Jesus Christ in the Most Holy Sacrament of the Altar.

May the sovereign will of God, most just and most amiable, be accomplished in all things; may it be praised and exalted for ever. Amen.

PATER. AVE. GLORIA.

Blessed be the Holy and Immaculate Conception of the Blessed Virgin Mary.

Remember, O most gracious Virgin Mary, that never was it known that anyone who fled to thy protection, implored thy help, or sought thy intercession, was left unaided. Inspired with this confidence, I fly unto thee, O Virgin of virgins, my Mother; to thee I come, before thee I stand, sinful and sorrowful; O Mother of the Word Incarnate, despise not my petitions; but in thy clemency hear and answer me. Amen.

O Mary, conceived without stain of original sin, pray for us who have recourse to thee. Amen.

First Night.

THE ANGELUS BELL.

The Angelus Bell.

CHAPTER I.

> "She has gone from us for ever,
> She has faded like the flowers,
> But she's gone to bloom unfading
> In a brighter land than ours."

"PLEASE don't ask me to play this evening, Ethel," said a young girl, pleadingly, as she sat down on one of the large square stones that skirted the terrace steps in the beautiful old convent garden.

"Why, what's the matter with you, Camille?" said her friend, anxiously scanning the wan little face before her.

"Oh, nothing, only these 'Compositions of Three' make me *so* tired, and I get such a pain here," and she laid her hand on her left side, "when I hear a question which I cannot answer; and I do *so* thirst for knowledge. I want to learn ever so much; but sometimes my head aches so, and I cannot."

"Then why do you trouble about it, Camille? What's the good of addling one's brains over a dull old lesson; after all, it's not *learning* that will bring us to heaven. When I've a headache, and it's often I find it convenient to have one, I just go up and ask the mistress of the study if I may go to the Infirmary. Of course she never refuses; and so I exchange my hard little stool for the comfortable arm-chair, and my wearisome 'Grammaire' for the delights of Miss Proctor."

"Ah, but Ethel, you don't understand: *I* do it all to please my Father."

"Your Father! Oh, nonsense."

Just then the ball hit Ethel, and the cry *brulée* made her run far away to the other end of the Cours; and Camille was left to her own sad reflections. Sad did I say; ah, yes, poor child, they *were* sad. It wanted but a fortnight to the end of the scholastic year; the last "Composition of Three" had been written that day; and somehow, much as Camille had tried, and hard as she had studied, she felt instinctively that her places would not be high; and as she had said to Ethel, she "*did* so thirst for knowledge."

Camille West was a Child of Mary, and fifth blue ribbon. I, too, was a Child of Mary, but far below her in the ribbons; we did not often speak to each other, which is not to be wondered at, since there were a hundred and eighty in the school. But this glorious July evening I sat not far away from her. I had sprained my ankle, and so was not obliged to play; and seeing the far-away, dreamy look in her eyes, I could not resist the temptation to go up and say playfully:

"A penny for your thoughts, Camille."

"My thoughts," she said; "they were scarcely worth a penny just at that moment, for they were envious ones."

"Why?" I asked, almost involuntarily.

"Oh, because I am wishing I could learn as easily as Alix Trémont, or Marie de St. Jean; they always know their lessons, and yet they never seem to learn them, and I am sure they will divide the first places in all these last compositions."

"Never mind, Camille," I said, consolingly; "I wouldn't give a fig for the way they learn their lessons; as soon as class is over I don't suppose they could remember ten words of the morning's work, while it's the plodders who retain everything. With the first 'it's lightly won and lightly lost;' while with such as you it's 'hard won, hard held,' don't you see."

"Yes, but I seem to make so little progress; and I do so long to learn a great deal, it's the one master-thought of my life to store up all the knowledge I possibly can."

"But, Camille," I said, "why do you work so hard?—you must have some object in view. Are you going to pass the examinations?"

"I do it all to please my Father," she said, simply. "Ah, there's the Angelus Bell; let us say it together."

It was Saturday evening, and so with folded hands and bowed heads we two children of the Sacred Heart stood at the feet of *Virgo Fidelis* and said that sweetest of Catholic prayers. Camille had asked me to give it out; and when I came to the words *Ecce ancilla Domini*, I saw her hands twitch convulsively, and her voice seemed to answer more earnestly: *Fiat mihi secundum verbum tuam.*

When we had finished, we turned, and with her hand on my shoulder, we walked slowly up the garden.

"Isn't the Angelus a sweet, comforting prayer," said Camille. "I always imagine I can see our Blessed Mother as she was when the angel appeared to her, kneeling at her *Prie-Dieu*, in deep meditation, while Gabriel comes down in a cloud of light and says: *Ave Maria.* I don't know how it is, but it seems to mean more when we say it in Latin."

"Ah, that's easily understood; Latin, you know, is the language of the Church, and therefore it sounds sweeter to her children than even their native tongue."

"How fortunate you are to be called Mary? I often wish my name were Mary."

"Why didn't you take it at Confirmation, then?" I asked.

"I don't know," she answered; "but I think it must have been because I had not then any deep devotion and love for the Blessed Virgin; I always loved her, you know; but not like I do now; and so at Confirmation I took the names of Theresa Madeleine—those are my two favourite saints."

"How strange!" I said; "they are mine, too; next to St. Joseph, my patron. If I had time I would tell you a story about St. Joseph and St. Peter, one, I think, that would make you laugh;

but here we are just at the refectory door, and so I cannot."

"Come to-morrow during mid-day recreation. I want to talk more about the Blessed Virgin; and I am so glad to have found someone who will listen to me."

"All right," I answered; "but you'll be going to the *salon*, won't you?"

"Oh, no," she said; "mamma is ill, and papa cannot leave her."

"Very well," I replied. And with this pact we separated, and went to our different places in the refectory.

I have told you that Camille West was a Child of Mary, and that her thoughts were often sad; but I have not told you what was saddest of all about her. She had an internal disease, which was eating her young life away; no one could tell how much she suffered; and yet she bore all patiently, never complaining except of a headache, and only too glad to have her sufferings to offer to the Blessed Virgin. I think I *never* knew or heard of anyone with such a devotion to *Mater Admirabilis;* she used to carry a little picture of her about with her, and I have seen her take it out of her little Manual, when she thought nobody was looking, and caress it with such reverential love that I have felt ashamed of my own lukewarmness.

Next day, Sunday, if I had forgotten my engagement, I don't think Camille would have let me; for no sooner was the signal given, and the *rangement* formed into their respective camps than she came up and said, laughingly:

"Come, Mary, let's take 'a little walk, a pleasant talk,' but unfortunately, it cannot be upon 'the briny beach;' and, moreover, I don't intend to eat you up when I've got all I want out of you, like the walrus and carpenter did to the poor oysters."

"I'm afraid I should prove an unsavoury morsel if you did," I answered. "Just look, Camille," I continued, "how rudely Marthe kicks the ball; really she ought to be black-balled."

"*You* ought to be black-balled, Miss, *pour avoir manqué à la charité.*"

"*Peccavi,*" I cried. "Come, let's flee temptation;—we were talking about the Angelus last night, weren't we?"

"Yes, and you promised to tell me a story about St. Joseph and St. Peter; don't you remember?"

"Oh, of course. Well, some years ago, my aunt, who is a Benedictine nun, and whose name in religion is Mother Mary Joseph, asserted one day at community recreation that St. Joseph was the greatest saint in heaven.

"'Not greater than St. Peter,' answered the mother-assistant, whose name was Bridget Peter.

"'Yes, greater even than St. Peter,' said Aunt Joseph.

"'Oh, but I say he's not,' returned Mother Peter, laughingly.

"'Ah, well, here's Father James,' said the Rev. Mother; 'he will decide the matter. Here, Father,' she said, as the parish priest came out of the house, 'here are two of your spiritual daughters disputing whether St. Joseph or St. Peter is greater in heaven, and I leave you to settle it between them.'

"'That's an easy affair,' replied Father James, who was a regular Irishman for wit and humour; 'and I'll prove it to you by an anecdote. You all know that St. Joseph was very much given to meditation, don't you? Well, one night he stayed out in the fields meditating, and was rather later than usual. When he came to the door of heaven and asked for admittance, St. Peter said he could not let him in, as he was late, and he had locked the door for the night. In vain did St. Joseph plead forgetfulness, St. Peter was inexorable. At last St. Joseph said quietly, but firmly: 'Then hand me out my Wife and Child, if you won't let me in.' It was the last straw, and St. Peter without a word opened the door, and let St. Joseph in; for,' ends the story, 'what would heaven be without Our Lord and Our Lady?'"

"How ridiculous," said Camille, laughing. "In the first place I did not know that St. Peter lived with the Holy Family."

"Oh, that I cannot explain," I said; "I only tell you the story as it was told to me. However, it proves, doesn't it, that St. Joseph *is* the greatest in heaven of all the saints?"

"I don't suppose anyone ever doubted it," she replied; "but the Blessed Virgin," she went on, closing her eyes; "O Mary, my Mother, if I could only make everyone love and honour you just a little, that little would lead them to greater things."

"I wish you would tell me the secret of your great devotion, Camille," I said.

"I don't think I could," she answered; "indeed there is no secret in it at all; only that she is so good to me, her unworthy child. 'Thy name, O Mary, is like oil poured out.' I seem to feel her influence in everything and everywhere; even when the studies are very hard, I know she helps me, and it's due to her the little I *can* do. Shall I tell you something, Mary?" she added, turning suddenly to me.

"Yes, if you like, dear," I answered; "only if it's something you think it better not to tell, don't mind giving me a share in it; somehow, I don't believe in school-girl confidences."

"Oh, it's nothing of *that* kind," she answered: "only I thought I would explain to you why I thirst so for knowledge, and why I put such entire confidence in the Blessed Virgin."

"Oh, then, if it's that, please do tell me, Camille," I said.

"Well, when I was made a Child of Mary, nearly two years ago, I asked Almighty God either to let me be a Sacred Heart Nun and go out to the missions, or else to let me die young; and from that day I took the resolution to learn with all my soul and with all my strength everything that I possibly could, and never to let slip an opportunity either of doing good or of gaining knowledge, so that I might be useful, if God did grant me the desire of my heart: but," she added, sorrowfully, "I am afraid He is going to take the alternative and let me die young; for very soon after that day, I began to feel this fearful pain in my side, and ever since it has never left me for long together; that is why I thirst so for knowledge, and that is why I say so fervently *Fiat mihi secundum verbum tuum* in the Angelus at morning, noon, and at eventide. I daresay you wondered last night, why I said, I worked so hard 'to please my Father:' *now* you understand, don't you, that I meant my Heavenly Father, and though I *do* love papa, very, very much, I am sure I should please *him* much better if I did *not* work so hard. He will not let me come back next year on that account; I have pleaded and coaxed, but in vain; he will not hear of it. Are *you* coming back, Mary?"

"I think so, I hope so," I answered. "But I shall miss you very much, Camille; I will write to you sometimes if you like, and give you news of the dear old place."

"Thanks, a thousand times, it would give me *such* pleasure. I know I shall regret my happy, happy schooldays; even mamma, sometimes says she wishes she were a child again and back at her desk in St. Madeleine."

CHAPTER II.

NINE months had passed away. It was the Feast of the Annunciation, and being a "double of second class," we had sermon and Benediction in the evening. Mons. l'Abbé chose for his text *Fiat mihi secundum verbum tuum*, and it seemed to fit in very exactly with some spiritual aspirations of my own.

The sun was streaming in through the stained-glass windows above the altar, glorifying St. Agatha and St. Cecilia, whom they represented, and glaring so unmercifully in my face that I was obliged to shade my eyes with my hand; and thus in a position, I fear more comfortable than reverential, I listened to our good chaplain's sermon—listened, but I am afraid *not* all the time. It was a distraction, against which I ought to have fought, but somehow I allowed my thoughts to wander away to Camille, the words of her favourite prayer, *Fiat mihi secundum verbum tuum*, I suppose, making me think of her more than I should have done.

As she had said, her father did not let her return to school: indeed the decision, unhappily, did not lie with him; for, during the long vacation, the disease which had hitherto been doing its work quietly began to show itself outwardly, and ever since, during nine long weary months, Camille had been laid on a bed of suffering, without scarcely a moment's alleviation.

I was wondering this evening, as we sat in chapel listening to the sermon, whether she were suffering less than usual just then. Poor child, she frequently sent messages to the convent; at one time it would be to tell the nuns how grateful she was to them for making her a Child of Mary; her medal, she said, was *such* a consolation to her; at another it would be to ask the children to pardon and forget any bad example she might have set them; again, it would be to beg some little memento of the House—a flower that had been on Our Lady's altar, or a medal which had come from Lourdes. The Mothers told us how ill she was, and asked us to pray that she might have grace and strength to bear her terrible sufferings; they told us of the long sleepless nights she passed in offering her pains to the Sacred Heart through the Blessed Virgin; and I think her example of patient resignation helped not a few of us to bear our minor little trials of school life.

Little did I think on this feast of our Immaculate Mother, that the same sun which was doing its best to blind me was trying vainly to pierce the French shutters of a room in a large Provençal city. The room was Camille's dressing-room, and on the couch drawn close up to her bedside she herself lay calmly, but with such a death-look on her face that it was impossible not to know that the "Angel" was very near, and that soon, very soon, Camille would be where she longed to be—with the Blessed Virgin for ever.

Mr. West was sitting watching by the couch, trying to remember, with agonising keenness, Camille's last words and wishes. "Papa," she said, presently, looking up. "I want you to read the 'Prayers for the Agonising;' but first I should like to give you a few messages and to bid mamma good-by;—Do you think she is strong enough to come over from her room? And, papa," she continued, as Mr. West rose up to fetch his wife, "I should not like mamma to know that it is good-bye, it would upset her.

Just say I'm sleepy and want to bid her good-night."

"Very well, darling," said her father, "I'll do as you wish."

"Camille is tired to-night, dear," he said to Mrs. West, "and says she thinks she could sleep; will you come and bid her good-night, she says she should like to see you if it would not tire you too much to come."

"Ah! that's a good sign," said her mother, rising from the sofa; "she's passed so many sleepless nights lately it will do her good, poor child."

"Mamma," said Camille, as Mrs. West came into her room, "it's a fancy; but I thought I should like to bid you good-night. I wanted to feel my earthly mother's arms round me—my heavenly Mother, you know, is always with me. She is so good to me, I can truly say, Her left arm is under my head, and Her right hand doth embrace me; but you, my earthly mother, are sick like myself, and so you cannot always be with me."

"No, my darling; but I will stay with you now until you fall asieep."

"*Please* don't, mother dear," said Camille. "Papa has promised to stay and read me to sleep, and you are not strong enough to sit up; please don't, mother," she pleaded.

"Very well, my child, it shall be as you wish," and Mrs. West left the sick-room to return to her couch. She loved Camille too tenderly and too well, and she knew that Camille loved her, her mother, too tenderly and too well not to be sure that it was love and self-forgetfulness which prompted the child to ask her mother to go away; but, ah, she did not, could not know that the end was so very near.

When his wife had gone, Mr. West resumed his vigil by the side of his only child. It was hard for him to let her go, but he was a truly Christian man, and had learned to say: "*Fiat voluntas tua, sicut in cælo et in terra,*" in the right spirit; and if his heart was faint, his religion made him strong in confidence and hope for this child, who since her birth had been to him as the "light of his eyes."

"Now, papa, for my messages," said Camille, almost brightly. "They are nearly all for the convent, with a love-word or two for Aunt Sophie and Uncle Mortimer. The messages for the nuns are the same as ever; tell them how grateful I am to them for all they have done for me, above all for making me a Child of Mary; tell them how sorry I am for all the trouble I gave them when at school; and, oh, papa, don't forget to ask Madame de Martini to tell the children to forget all my bad example, and to be sure and pray for me when I am gone; and then again, remember your promise that I should be dressed in my white uniform and blue ribbon just as a Sacred Heart Child, when—when—I am—dead. Now, papa, please, I think that is all; will you begin the 'Prayers for the Agonising,' I feel getting weaker and weaker?"

Mr. West did as Camille told him, though he required a strong effort to control his voice; and then in the awful stillness of that death-chamber he read those all-consoling prayers with which our Holy Mother the Church sends her children to their everlasting rest. Camille had made a general confession that day, and the Jesuit Father who had attended her during the worst periods of her illness had only left her that evening, because he thought she *looked* so much better. His last words to her father had been very comforting. "I think, Mr. West," he said, "that you have every ground for confidence for that dear child: I firmly believe she has never lost her baptismal innocence."

Mr. West had just began the Litany of the

Agonising, "St. Joseph, Spouse of the Blessed Virgin, pray for this soul," when Camille raised herself with an effort and said, feebly:

"Listen, papa, isn't that the Angelus Bell?"

"Yes, my darling; shall I say it?"

"Oh, please," she answered.

The replies to the first clause were distinct enough, and poor Mr. West thought perhaps she would rally; but when he said "*Ecce ancilla Domini,*" he could scarcely hear her answer, she said it so low and so slowly: "*Fiat—mihi—secundum—verbum.*"

There was no more: with a convulsive twitch at her precious medal, and a weary backward movement, Camille West sank to sleep—indeed, to sleep in the arms of the angel whom the Blessed Virgin had sent to bring her to Herself!

* * * * * * *

The next morning, as we were changing from the class-rooms to Ste. Madeleine, the great study-hall, we were surprised by the unusual sound of the signal for silence. It was the Mistress-General who used it, and at once nearly two hundred pairs of eyes were turned towards where she stood.

"Children," she said, gently, "I have come to ask you to pray for Camille West; last night at the Angelus Bell she died. Among her last requests was one that you would pray for her, and try to forget any bad example she might have given you; but that I am sure you can easily do, for she was always a good child and loved our dear Lord and his Blessed Mother devotedly."

"And so," I thought, sorrowfully, "God *had* taken the alternative, and let her die young, instead of granting her her soul's desire. Truly, His ways are not *our* ways, nor *His* thoughts *our* thoughts!"

Second Night.

SHORT LEGENDS AND ANECDOTES.

A Legend of Normandy.

DEAR little ones, you all know the beautiful story of the Passion. I would tell it to you to-night, for I could never tire of the wondrous history, only our half hour is so short, and we must remember that we have five little tales to hear in it.

Well, then, you must each make a prelude of the Way of the Cross. The great multitude had followed our dear Lord from Jerusalem, some in love and sorrow, others, alas! in mockery and derision. The awful work of man's redemption was completed—awful in more senses than one. Awful in the cruelty of the soldiers; awful in that the Crucified was not only our Redeemer, but also our Creator; awful in the stillness which reigned around; and awful in the events which accompanied it! Jesus, the King of heaven and earth, had given up the ghost, and was dead; but the Precious Blood still dripped slowly from His wounded Hands and Feet. A robin, then a simple little brown bird, came and perched on the left arm of the cross. His black eyes, usually so bright and clear, were dim now, as if he knew Who it was that hung there; he seemed to understand the cruelty of the Jews in *nailing* the Sacred Hands and Feet; and stooping down, he tried to draw out the left nail with his tiny, fragile beak. He could not, though; the sharp nail was stronger than he; and disappointed, he perched once more on the arm of the cross, gazing sorrowfully at the thorn-crowned head and sweet, patient face. He happened to look down at himself, too—why I cannot tell—and he found that some of the Precious Blood had fallen on his tiny bosom, and dyed it a deep, scarlet colour. This, then, is the cause—so they say in Normandy—why the dear little robin has a red breast.

And, dear little ones, may *we* not learn a lesson from this? May we not try to draw the nails out of the dear Hands and Feet of our most loving Lord by many acts of reparation to his Sacred

Heart; and, doing it, may we not truly not only hope, but be quite sure that the Precious Blood will fall on our bosoms also, and falling "wash us whiter than snow."

* * * * * * *

FAITH.

Listen to me now, children, for I am going to tell you a true story: one that a Jesuit Father told us during the Retreat when I was a school-girl.

Not many years ago there lived, in a large French town, a wealthy family, which consisted of father, mother, grandmother, and one little girl. Their beautiful house stood just without the city walls, and there in the old garden Marie (that was the little girl's name) would play on the long warm summer days; or, if the weather were cold, she had a large nursery all to herself. Rather lonely must it not have been, don't you think, without any little brothers and sisters? Somehow or other *I* always fall in with the old saying, "The more the merrier;" don't you?

Nevertheless, Marie was very happy; she had a good father and mother, who taught her to love the Sacred Heart and the Blessed Virgin; and it was wonderful to see the faith she had in the Blessed Sacrament. But a shadow was soon to fall on Marie's home: her dear mother fell ill, so ill that the doctors said she must die; and this made Marie's grandmother very sad. She had been watching beside her daughter, who had now fallen asleep, and she thought she would just go into the nursery and prepare Marie for the great sorrow she knew must soon come to her: for Marie did not know how *very* ill her mother was.

She stole quietly into the nursery, then, where her little grandchild was playing with her dolls: she had them all seated in a row before her, and was pretending to teach them their catechism.

"Marie, *ma petite*," said Madame de Beaucœur, taking her on her knee, "do you know that your mamma is very ill?"

"Very ill, is she, grandmamma?" said Marie, looking up into Madame de Beaucœur's face.

"Yes, very ill; so ill that perhaps the good God may send an angel to take her away from us altogether. Won't you pray, Marie, that God may make her better?"

"I will," replied Marie, thoughtfully.

Her grandmother wondered she did not cry; and left the nursery as quietly as she had come in. Marie, too, did not remain long behind her;

she was an only child, and allowed to roam about the large house as she pleased; so the nurse did not hinder her when she went away. She went gently down stairs, with her finger on her lip, as if she were either afraid of disturbing her mother or else as if she were thinking very deeply. She met the butler in the entrance-hall, and he thought to himself: "Dear me, how good Miss Marie is; she is so quiet and thoughtful while her mamma is so ill;" and then he went on into his pantry. But Marie took her garden hat off the peg, and gently unlatched the halldoor, and then step by step she went down the deep white stone stairs. Once outside the garden gate, she looked back cautiously to make sure that no one was following her; and then as fast as ever she could she ran, and never stopped until she reached a neighbouring church, which stood about three hundred yards from the house. Taking some holy water, she went inside. There was no one there; but that was just what Marie wanted. She waited at the door, and said, in a timid voice, though loud enough to be heard: "Jesus, are you there?" and then with her finger on her lip and her head bent, she listened for an answer. But no answer came: so she went further into the church, and about half way up the aisle she repeated: "Jesus, are you there?" Still there was no answer. But Marie was not discouraged, and she advanced still further until she reached the altar rails, and then again she said, "Jesus, are you there?" Each time she had spoken a little louder than the last, but as before she only heard the echo of her own little voice. There was but one thing more to do, and Marie did it. Climbing over the rails into the sanctuary, she dragged the chair which stood behind the *prie-dieu*, where the priest made his thanksgiving, up the altar-steps, and placing it firmly upon the ground, she mounted it, and knocked ever so gently at the door of the Tabernacle! "Jesus, are you there?" she whispered, as if afraid of her own faith. But this time she *was* answered. She heard, as it were, a voice in her heart, which said: "Go home, little girl, your mamma is cured." She waited not a minute; but, replacing the chair, she ran home as quickly as she had come, and went back into the nursery as if nothing extraordinary had happened.

Presently her grandmother came back again, with a bright, glad face. "Marie, *ma petite*," she said, "be happy and gay; your mamma is cured;—are you not glad?"

"Yes; but I don't wonder at it: I asked Jesus

to make her well, and He said He would," replied Marie, simply.

And then Madame de Beaucœur drew from her little grandchild the story of her great Faith: and comparing the time of her daughter's miraculous recovery, she found it to be exactly the moment when Marie had heard that strange, sweet voice deep down in her little heart! So you see how Marie's faith was rewarded. And once more, dear little ones, shall we not imitate Marie? and if we feel lonely, sometimes, it may be in the dark, or we may be left alone, or the devil may tempt us to do and say wrong things; but shall we not always say, "Jesus, are you there?" And be sure, that as He answered Marie, so He will come to your aid; for nobody ever yet called for Him, really and truly wishing Him to come to them, but He did come, and that quickly and without delay!

* * * * * * *

And now will you listen to another story that good father told us during the same Retreat. He was a French Jesuit, so all his tales happened in his native land—France. You all know where Auvergne is, don't you? Well, it is far away down in the middle of the South of France. That is a queer sentence, is it not; but still it explains my meaning. There are a great many forests in Auvergne; but on the borders of one particular forest there was a village, and the people who lived there were poor, very poor, and it was called Mont St. Jean. In one of the many little cottages which composed it there lived a poor widow with six children, and she earned her bread by knitting stockings and vests, and by spinning flax and wool. She loved the Blessed Virgin very, very much, and she spent as much time as she could spare from her work every day in saying her Rosary in the village chapel before an image of "Our Lady of Perpetual Help," which, as you know, represents our dear and holy Mother with the Infant Jesus in her arms.

Marthe Besson's faith and trust in the Blessed Virgin's power were so great, that without a thought she told Our Lady that she depended solely on her to look after and mind her little children, as they played around in the village; that she, Marthe, had to earn their bread, so that she trusted to their Mother in heaven to shield them from all danger. Marthe loved all her children very dearly, but especially did she love the youngest, a chubby baby-boy, three years old;—but a trial to her Faith was coming, and this was how it happened:

One morning in early spring, as Marthe was sitting spinning, a neighbour rushed into her cottage, exclaiming: "But, Mother Besson, do you not know your little Louis has been carried off by a wolf. Arise, then, and let us run after him, and rescue your baby."

But instead of beginning to scream, or rushing out of her house, as the kind-hearted neighbour had rushed in, Marthe quietly laid aside her distaff, and rising leisurely, reached her shawl from its nail. Throwing it about her shoulders, she left the cottage, and to Maurice Langle's great surprise she took the opposite direction to the forest, and walked quickly towards the village church. Arrived there, she went straight up to the statue of Our Lady, and with holy boldness snatched the Infant Jesus out of her arms. "When you have given me back mine, then I will restore you yours," she said; and then left the chapel with her precious burden in her arms. When she reached her cottage she placed the Image beside her, while she resumed her work, without so much as an anxious thought for the safety of her child.

The morning had passed, and the afternoon was waning apace, and still no sign of little Louis had been discovered. All his brothers and sisters were out aiding in the search; but his mother never once left her work, for she *knew*, somehow, that the Blessed Virgin would keep her baby safe. Nor did she believe in vain. The band of seekers whom Monsieur le Curé had sent out to look for the little lost lamb was just going to give up the search as useless, when one of them saw, or thought he saw, something unusual afar off under a spreading pine-tree. He was right: for on coming nearer he discovered Mother Besson's little baby with its golden head resting on a dark-brown wolf's body, and both were fast asleep. But how to rescue the child was a perplexity which presented itself to poor Jean: if he snatched Louis away, the wolf would awake and attack himself; he could only think of one thing to do, and that was to stab the animal. You see he couldn't help it, could he? So, taking his long, sharp knife, he thrust it deep into the wolf's side, at the same time seizing the baby in his arms. The wolf got up, but finding itself wounded, gave a fearful yell, and fell back dead. Jean now made haste back to the village with the glad news that he had found Louis, whom he restored to Marthe. Mother Besson kissed her baby, and bidding him be careful to keep with his little brothers and sisters in future, she once more set out for the village church; but this time with the Image of the Holy Child in her arms.

"It is well that you have restored me mine," she said to the Blessed Virgin, as she replaced the Infant Jesus; "without that, you should not have had *yours* back again." And she returned to her work again with the same great trust in Our Lady's care of her children that she had always had.

* * * * * * *

The story which I am going to tell you now is one which I heard a great many years ago myself, and as I have a very shaky memory I cannot be quite sure of its correctness; however, I will do my best to tell it aright, and after this frank confession of my weakness you will forgive me any little errors, I know.

"Once upon a time, then, as Baby Veronica likes me to begin my stories, once upon a time, there lived a great and powerful prince—I do not remember his name; but with all his riches and lands, he was not happy because of them. Like Marthe Besson, in the last tale, he loved Our Blessed Lady very much, indeed, and was very fond of saying the *Ave Maria;* so what do you think he did? He got a little canary bird, whom, after a great deal of pains and trouble, he taught to speak, and to say, *"Ave Maria, gratia plena, Dominus tecum."* So the little bird kept on saying all day long his little prayer, and scarcely ever stopped. One day, however, he got tired of his golden cage, and of being shut up; so, finding the door of his little house open, he flew out of the window, far, far, ever so far away. But at last he got very weary: he had never been used to fly about much, and this long journey had tired him a great deal; so he perched on the ivy-grown wall of an old ruined church, and as soon as he recovered his breath, he began his little prayer, *"Ave Maria, gratia plena, Dominus tecum."*

It was getting quite dark now, for, as you know, the winter days are very short, and Dickie thought he should be frozen if he slept on the broken-down old wall all night; so he took wing again and flew on, on, on, until he saw a grove of trees, in which he felt sure he should find a shelter. He reached it at last, and found it was full of a great many different kinds of birds, quite different to what he himself was: for *they* were brown and black, and speckled, and red-breasted, while he was of a lovely golden colour. He found, too, that they were all just singing a good-night song to each other before curling themselves up to sleep in their tiny nests: so Master Dickie began his little song also, and trolled out "*Ave Maria, gratia plena, Dominus tecum.*" The other birds were too sleepy that night to notice that his notes were strange and quite different to theirs, so they let him go quietly to rest: no one asked him to share his nest, though, and so, poor little fellow, he had to perch on the top of a tall tree, and bury himself as much as he could in the thick leaves which he found there. But about six o'clock the next morning, when the other little birds began to open their bright, beady eyes, he too rose up, and shook out his wings: he even had the courage to hop down a branch or two lower, so as to be more sociable, and then he began, as he always did, the first thing in the morning, his little prayer, "*Ave Maria, gratia plena, Dominus tecum.*" The other birds were wide awake now, and not at all too sleepy to notice his strange plumage and still stranger voice. They looked at each other, and seemed as if by one consent to agree to chase our poor little friend from their cosy grove, which they considered as quite private property; so they all, or at least a great many of them, collected on the tree on which Dickie was perched, and began teasing and tormenting him. Was not that unkind? He was getting frightened, poor little fellow, and began to flutter, and to turn his head from side to side, as if seeking some means of escape. At last he took courage, and being fleeter of wing than his hosts, he flew away, away, until he saw the prince's castle, and his own home like a black speck in the distance: and I can tell you he was not at all sorry to see the turrets and the watch-towers, as every minute he drew nearer and nearer. He had almost reached the castle walls, nay, he could even make out his own golden cage standing in the dining-room window, with the door open, ready to receive him, whenever it should please him to return, when he saw a great big "something" high up in the air above his head. The big "something" grew bigger and bigger to his poor little imagination: he could see its immense claws now, ready to seize him, as it swooped down upon him and caught him as its prey. Suddenly he screamed out "*Ave Maria, gratia plena, Dominus tecum,*" and at that moment the hawk—for it was one—fell dead on the ground, shot by the prince's own gun. The prince did not know, though, that he was very nearly shooting his own dear little canary when he fired that shot. And I leave you to imagine his delight when he came home that night and found Dickie asleep in his cage, standing on one foot, while the other was tucked up snugly under his wing.

And now, dear little ones, you see how the Blessed Virgin helps those who call upon her and trust in her. You see how she even saved from death a poor little bird, who said *"Ave Maria, gratia plena, Dominus tecum"* when he was frightened. And if you call upon her like that she will hear and help you, too; for I cannot tell you how she loves to hear little children singing her praises: I almost think she loves it better than those of big people.

* * * * * * *

MATER ADMIRABILIS.

"The rose was in rich bloom on Sharon's plain,
When a young mother with her first-born
Thence went up to Sion. By the hand she led her,
And her silent soul the while, rejoiced to think
That ought so pure, so beautiful was hers,
To bring before her God."

These lines were written by the great poetess, Mrs. Hemans, but they suit so well what I am going to tell you about our dear and holy *Mater Admirabilis* that I have used them. Yes, St. Anne was bringing up her little daughter to

Jerusalem, there to dedicate her to the service of God. It was by her own wish that she was thus leaving her home and her parents. She was only three years old, yet she heard God's call so distinctly, and hearing it, obeyed it so promptly, that now she was on her way to the Holy City.

"At last the fane was reached—the earth's one sanctuary—
And rapture hushed her bosom, as before her thro' the wild
It rose, a mountain of white glory, steeped in light,
Like floating gold."

I do not know, children, if you quite understand these words; but to me they had a deep meaning when I learnt them long ago, while making my fourth class, and as I was only nine years old then, I have written them, thinking and hoping they may have the same meaning for you.

Yes, there it stood, the beautiful Temple to which St. Anne was bringing her child. It must have been a great trial to her to part with her. She was *such* a good little daughter. She had never disobeyed her father or mother even once. How could she?—for, as you know, "she had no sin in her." But when the time came to say good-bye, her mother could bear up no longer, and "bending o'er her child, her soul broke forth in mingled sounds of weeping and sad song."

> " 'Alas, my child,' she cried, ' alas ! and must I leave thee,
>   How the lone paths retrace, where thou wert playing
> So late along the mountains at my side,
>   And I in joyous pride, at every place of flowers, my steps delaying,
> Wove e'en as pearls, the lilies round thy hair,
> Beholding thee so fair !' "

The little child did all she could to comfort her mother, telling her that she had come to serve God, and that He would comfort her and guard her. Then she ran with outstretched arms to the venerable High-Priest, who was awaiting her, and thus did *Mater Admirabilis* begin her life in the Temple. Of course you know that the Jews in building their Temples, always keep one place sacred, into which *no one* but the High-Priest may enter, and even he must go through a great many outward forms of cleansing himself before he can do so. Don't you remember when Moses was told to make the "Ark of the Covenant," while the children of Israel were still wandering in the wilderness, how God told him to build also a "Holy of Holies?" Well, just the same, there was a "Holy of Holies" in the Temple at Jerusalem, and *Mater*

Admirabilis was found so pure, and so good, and so holy, that she was let go in there. Only think! into the place which was but a type or figure of the Tabernacle in which our dear Lord remains always in all our churches.

But our dear Mother had much to suffer while she remained in the Temple; there were some other children there, too, not half as good as she, who were envious and jealous because she did all she had to do so perfectly; and one night they had a competition in needlework to see who could do it the best. The embroidery was to be given in to be judged next day, and so these naughty children got up and undid all the Blessed Virgin's piece, because they knew that *she* would get the prize. But God meant her to get the reward: it did not matter to Him that her enemies had spoiled her work; so He sent a lovely shining angel, who did it all over again, just as it was before; so you see *Mater Admirabilis got* the prize after all!

There are a great many more things told of this most perfect child while she was in the Temple; but I want to tell you why we Sacred Heart children love and honour her so much, under the name *Mater Admirabilis*.

Many years ago some of our Mothers were

sitting working in the community room at Rome, when Rev. Mother was called away on business to another part of the house.

"Oh, how I wish," said one of the nuns, "that the Blessed Virgin could come and sit in Rev. Mother's place!"

"Shall I make her come, then?" said a young postulant—that is, a person who wants to become a nun; but who must pass some time in the convent before she can wear the dress.

"I wish you could; but you cannot," they said.

But she was not afraid; and getting Rev. Mother's permission, she set to work to paint Our Blessed Lady after a thought of her own. She did it in fresco, which is a kind of painting done on wet plaster; and when she had finished it, it looked *so* ugly, one mass of gaudy, unsightly colours. And Rev. Mother said it must be destroyed; so a man who knew all about such things was called in to pull it down; but he begged so hard that it might remain—at least until it was dry—that Rev. Mother consented; so it was covered up for about three weeks, or perhaps a little longer. Then the painter came, and took off the cover, and, oh, what a *lovely* picture was there! Our Blessed Lady was seated in a paved court of

The Gift the Christ-Child brought.

"Old Christmas has a way of making people jolly,
He brings such bright array of mistletoe and holly!
He echoes through the earth like joybells thro' a steeple,
And wakens fun and mirth within the gravest people."
EDEN HOOPER.

IT was not hard to tell that it was winter, nor yet to tell that Christmas had arrived—Christmas, with its holly and mistletoe; Christmas, with its bright faces and cheery voices; Christmas, with its plum-puddings and turkeys; but, best of all, Christmas as we keep it in memory of the dear Lord, Who came down to earth so many hundred years ago, there to be despised and poor for our sakes, and Who now only waits and watches to come again into our hearts, if we will only receive Him. Many things besides all I have mentioned told eager little hearts and the owners of longing little eyes, that the long-looked-forward-to Christmas had come! The crisp white snow outside, that lay six inches deep on the ground; the keen winter air that nipped certain little noses and ears so tormentingly; and then down in the town the brilliantly lighted shops, whose windows displayed such wondrous treasures. I am not sure that I did not see famous Santa Claus flying over the roofs of certain houses in his fairy chariot drawn by two white cats; or dear old Father Christmas himself with his red coat and long snowy beard, stopping at a great many places to buy lots of things with which he loaded his already well-freighted and patient old donkey. At any rate, if I only saw these two good old men in imagination, I *know* I saw a great many fathers and mothers flitting about in the old town of Harnet, chiefly between the toy-shops and the confectioners.

I was walking briskly down High-street, comfortably wrapped up in my fur-lined cloak, when I noticed a poor little girl looking very wistfully into a cake-shop where the smell of sundry mince-pies called out most loudly to passers-by to look in and taste them. I cannot tell what made me slacken my steps as I passed this little girl; but I *don't* think it was the smell of the mince-pies, as I never did care very much for them; nor yet can I tell what moved me to turn back, after I had left her and the cake-shop a good way behind: it certainly was not because I had a great deal of time to spare, for I was in a hurry, and besides the keen winter air was biting *my* nose and ears as well as those of some of my little friends.

I found the little girl where I had left her, still gazing wistfully through the plate-glass which separated her from the object of her desires.

"My child," I said, gently laying my hand on her shoulder, "why do you stand there? Don't you find it very cold?"

The poor little creature turned her large blue eyes slowly from the window, and fixed them sorrowfully upon me. Her look cut me to the heart, it had such a depth of patient, unmurmuring endurance in it, and the thought flashed across me, how many were going to spend this holy Christmas-tide in starvation and misery!

"No, ma'am," she answered, "it's not cold here; the fire below warms me, and I like to watch the ladies and gentlemen inside."

"Have you no money, then," I asked, "to buy something like they are doing?"

"Oh, ma'am," she said, sobbingly, "mother *is* so ill; and I was just thinking how much she would like that little pie. I came out to beg, but—but I think shame to!"

"Tell me, my poor child," I said, "what ails your mother, and where do you live?"

"Oh, mother's very sick, and father died a month ago; before that we used to get on very well: mother took in washing, and father worked for Hanby the builder; but then he died, and the landlord turned us out, and now we live in Angel Court, No. 4, in the top attic."

"And is there no one living with you?"

"No, ma'am; only mother and myself."

"And my child," I questioned, "of what religion are you?"

The little girl hesitated. I saw she was debating in her own mind, and asking herself of what religion *I* was. But grace and the deep and true love which all Catholics have and feel for their Holy Faith gained the mastery, and she answered unflinchingly: "Mother has been a Catholic a long time, ma'am, long and long before I was born. She says now, that if she were not, she could not bear up under all the trials the Lord is sending her. Father Haynes often comes in to see her, and he does all he can to help us. He said last week he would ask a young lady he knew to come in and see us too."

"Did he tell you the young lady's name, or do you remember it?" I asked, guessing pretty well that "Father Haynes' young lady" was myself.

"Miss Cra—Cra—oh, I can't remember it, ma'am; but it was something like that."

"Was it Miss Craven, do you think, my poor child?"

"Oh, yes, that was it; Father Haynes said she loved the poor very much, and did a great deal of good, and he told mother she would be sure to be kind to her; but," she added, sadly, "I'm afraid he's forgotten to tell Miss Craven about us, and when he drops in I don't like to remind him."

"Well, never mind, my child," I said; "Miss Craven knows all about you; let's see and get some supper for you and your mother, and then run home and tell her Miss Craven is coming to see her to-morrow; do you understand?"

"Oh, yes, Miss; and please, Miss, are *you* Miss Craven?"

"You've given a good guess; yes, I *am* Miss Craven. Now come along and show me what you think your mother would like best; but first tell me your name, or else I shan't know who to seek to-morrow when I go to Angel-court."

"Mary Stephens, ma'am, and mother's name is the same."

"Very well—'Mary Stephens'—I must try and remember;—and it's No. 4 Angel-court, you say?"

"Yes, ma'am; in the top attic; and please, ma'am, excuse my boldness, but you'll want to mind coming up the stairs, for they're *very* rickety."

"Thanks, I'll recollect," I said. "Now I'm afraid you must buy your supper yourself; you can, can't you? Because I am in a great hurry and must make haste home again."

And with a cheery good-night I continued my way with a heart lighter and happier for having eased the burden of a fellow-creature.

My errand took me quite to the other end of High-street; it was to ask a lady would she kindly lead the choir on Christmas Day for my sister. Harnet was an eminently Protestant town; so our dear old parish priest had a very small cure of souls, and a very poor one besides, and this was the reason why my sister took the choir, and another lady volunteered to play the harmonium, and yet another insisted on relieving

Father Haynes of the care of the little church; and this devotion and love for our pastor drew us all together in a more kindly way than any amount of social visiting could do, I think.

I was just making an offering of my disappointment at not finding Mrs. Eden at home, when I met her coming in at her own gate.

"A thousand times well met!" I cried. "I was nearly having a long cold walk for nothing!"

"I'm sorry for that," she answered, pleasantly. "Won't you come in?"

"Oh, no, thanks," I said; "I've already loitered too long, I've only come to ask if you'll have the charity to take the choir for Edith on Christmas Day; she is suffering so acutely from neuralgia, and when once it begins with her she has to put up with it for a long time, as she says herself, it must wear itself out!"

"I'll take the singing with pleasure, Miss Craven," said Mrs. Eden; "but I may count on your help, may I not?"

"Ah, that I'm afraid you must not do; I shall go to early Mass, as I cannot leave Edith alone, unless, indeed, mamma should arrive to-morrow; but I shall be able to let you know that. Could you come up to tea with us to-morrow evening?"

"I'm sorry to have to refuse; but my boys are

coming home from school, and I could not be out when they arrive, could I?"

"Indeed you could not," I replied; "however, *cela s'arrangera*. Good-bye!"

"Good-night, Miss Craven," returned Mrs. Eden, disappearing behind her own hall-door.

I almost ran all the way back to Westfield. My sister was naturally of a nervous temperament, and my long and unwonted absence would be sure to worry her. The lights of the town had ceased to glimmer across my path, when I was startled by a voice exclaiming:

"You here! What on earth brings you out at this hour of the night?"

In an instant I recognised the voice: it belonged to Father Haynes, and I answered, laughing, "An errand of charity and a deed of mercy, both together; and *apropos* of that last, though I know it's disrespectful to accuse one's superiors, still I have an accusation to bring against you, Father! You never told me about your *protegées*, Mary Stephens, senior, and Mary Stephens, junior!"

"I plead guilty," said the priest; "but how did you come to know about them?"

"By one of those accidents which happen every day. She was eyeing the cakes in a shop window, and I was attracted by her wistful expression, and so the thought was father to the act, and I stepped up and got to know all about her. I promised to go and see her mother to-morrow."

"That's a good little maid," said the Father.

"Oh, won't you come in?" I said, as we reached Westfield-gate.

"I can't, I'm sorry to say: it's a sick-call, and I must not delay."

"Good-night, then, Father; remember you've promised to dine here on Christmas Day; and don't let other people cajole you into accepting their invitations by forgetting ours?"

"There's not much fear of that, Muriel; you know you are my child since you were a baby;—but good-night, you little witch, I believe you would keep me talking all night if you could!"

I was glad to get into my sister's warm home again, for the cold night air outside had had anything but an enlivening effect on my spirits, and then my thoughts had been sad because of poor little Mary Stephens and her mother.

I found my four-year-old nephew in the hall, playing hide-and-seek with his French *bonne* to evade being captured and led off to bed.

"Oh, auntie," he screamed, as he discovered

me wiping the snow off my boots, "*when will* old Father Christmas come and fill my stocking; I've had it hanging out for the last week and he's never come near it!"

"Oh, but you've hung it out too soon," I replied, "he won't come until to-morrow night, Christmas Eve."

"And do you think he'll bring me lots of things, auntie," he asked, naively.

"I don't know, I'm sure, Ralph," I answered; "wait till grannie comes to-morrow, and then ask *her*. Now run off, there's a treasure; see Marie, how patiently she is waiting for you. I must run in to your mamma; good-night, darling."

Edith was lying on a sofa when I entered the dining-room, but she rose and stirred the fire, and then seated herself in an arm-chair and told me to come and sit at her feet, as I used to do long ago before she was married.

"Is the pain better to-night, dear?" I said, when we were comfortably settled.

"Not much, Dot," she replied, using my familiar pet-name; "but why on earth did you go out on such a cold, raw night?"

"Only not to let the music fall through at second Mass for want of a leader," I said. "You know *you* can't go; so I just ran down to ask Mrs. Eden if she would have the charity to take your place, and she said she would. Her boys are coming home to-morrow; you ought to ask them up here some evening, they are such nice little fellows."

"Yes, we must get up some kind of a Christmas party for Ralph. I think we might even manage a 'tree,' don't you."

"That would be capital," I exclaimed; "I shan't have time to think about it until next week, though, I have so much to do housekeeping!"

"Poor little woman," said Edith, lovingly, "don't tire yourself too much."

"There's not any fear of that," I said, laughing; "you know what a selfish, self-contained little mortal I am. That remark about housekeeping was only a boast, I verily believe; at all events, I think that tea would be desirable at the present moment," I added, jumping up and ringing the bell; "perhaps Martha means us to starve because it's Christmas!"

The next day was ushered in as cold and as wet and as slushy as any misanthrope could wish; a heavy rain had fallen all night and had turned the crisp white snow to an uncomfortable mud stream, through which anyone whose business drew them away from their own fireside had to wade in order to accomplish it. I was sorely tempted to put off my visit to Mrs. Stephens. "At any rate," I thought, shiveringly, "I won't go till this afternoon: perhaps it may dry up a bit underfoot between now and then."

The afternoon proved far worse than the morning: a thin drizzling rain had begun, and the wind blew, as Martha said, "to cut the horns of a ram." But I had a very bad habit of scolding people for making promises and then breaking them, and I could not very well preach if I broke my own word now; so I ran upstairs and donned my ulster, and with a stout umbrella I issued forth to battle with the wind and rain, and to find Angel-court. Yes, to *find* Angel-court! for the melancholy fact presented itself to me that I knew no more than the man in the moon, perhaps even less, where Angel-court was! My instinct told me that I should find it sooner by making for High-street than by meandering up and down all the bye-lanes and alleys in the town, and so for High-street I steered.

Arrived there, not a human soul was visible from one end to the other; all the good folk of

Harnet had evidently been wise, and laid in their Christmas stores in good time. I turned into the first respectable shop I met, and asked if they could direct me to Angel-court.

"Angel-court!—Angel-court, Miss," answered the young man—"I never heard of such a place. Angel-court!—it must be some filthy locality down the back streets!"

"I daresay it is," I replied, "but such as it is I wish to find it; I am sorry you can't help me. Good-morning."

At the next turning I very nearly fell into the arms, or rather nearly knocked down with my open umbrella, a stalwart skipper, who, with his head bent, was cutting the wind like his own good little vessel.

"Can *you* tell me where Angel-court is?" I gasped between the gusts of wind.

"Angel-court, ma'am?" he exclaimed, rather incredulously.

"Yes, Angel-court," I said, impatiently, for I was getting tired of my quest, and was blaming myself unmercifully for not having made sure where Mary Stephens lived the night before.

"I guess you'll have to go a good many paces, ma'am; it's a long piece from this. Let's see. Mortimer-street, Preston-lane," and he went on mumbling to himself. "Take the fourth turning from this, Miss, on the other side, Huggermugger-lane it's called, and then go along it nearly to the end; you must ask your way there, for I'm not sure which way it runs."

"Thank you," I said, and hurried off once more in my miserable search.

I carefully counted the turnings, and arrived, as my good skipper had said, at Huggermugger-lane. Walking here was even more difficult than in High-street, and once or twice I was nearly blown off my feet. I had reached the end of the lane and not seen a single person, and but one filthy alley remained to be passed. Looking up to the name-board, I found to my great joy that it was called Angel-street; surely, I thought, Angel-court cannot be far from this; nor was it: a few more steps and I entered a dilapidated blind alley, and this I was informed by a lazy woman, standing in her doorway, was the object of my quest.

"Is this No. 4, then," I asked, counting the houses from the entrance.

"No, it's on t'other side," she answered, surlily."

So I crossed the filthy street and pushed open the door of No. 4, as I looked in vain for a knocker or bell wherewith to solicit admittance. All was dark in the apology for a hall, and I groped my way nervously to where I imagined the staircase must be. Mary Stephens, or "Little Meg," as she was commonly called in these parts to distinguish her from her mother, had not warned me needlessly about the unsteady condition of the stairs, and my only wonder is that I escaped without a broken limb. However, I landed safely at the top, and then saw what I supposed was Mrs. Stephens's attic. I knocked timidly at first, but receiving no answer I applied my knuckles more vigorously. Still no answer. Once more I rapped; but all inside was silent as the grave, and I was just turning away, terribly disappointed that my long, cold walk had been taken for nothing, when I heard a deep, unearthly groan which came from the attic. I was sure now that *somebody* was within, so I forced the door open; for Little Meg had secured it in some way, so that only she herself could open it without trouble, and then I entered the room. Let me just describe it as I remember it. Did I *ever* see such poverty, and yet withal such cleanliness!— such an attempt to save appearances, and to make the best of everything! My heart grew cold with pity, and self-abasement, and horror as I noted each thing one after another: the empty grate, the bottomless cane-chair, the scoured deal table—this was all the furniture the room boasted, save and except the straw pallet in the corner of the attic on which lay stretched a woman, motionless and pale as death, with her newly-born infant by her side. What was I, that I should be living at home in comfort, if not in affluence, while such misery was being endured, and so heroically endured, by another of God's creatures? But this was not the time for idle reflections. I felt I must act; and going over to the bed I laid my hand on the woman's pulse. It still beat; but I had nothing wherewith to restore her. Just at that moment her child came in with a sorrowful, disappointed face.

"Why did you leave your mother, Mary?" I said, reproachfully; "she is very ill."

"I know it, ma'am," answered the little girl; "I went out to ask someone to bury the baby; but—but—" she sobbed, "no one will!"

Up to this time I had not noticed the newcomer, and taking the poor little waif in my arms I found it was quite dead; but the mother's life might be saved, so I said hastily:

"Do you know where Dr. Murray lives, Mary?"

"Yes, ma'am; at the other end of High-street."

"Then run at once, as quick as ever your legs can carry you, and tell him Miss Craven wants him. Nay, stay! I'll just write him a line," I continued, as the thought struck me that the good old doctor might not heed the message without corroboration; so I took out a slip of paper and wrote: "Please come quickly to No. 4 Angel-court; I am in great distress. M. C." I knew Dr. Murray would come at once on getting this; for he was, like Father Haynes, a very dear old friend of mine.

Little Meg started off at once on her errand, and I sat down on the floor to wait and to watch in patience. I did not release my hold of the pulse, and it seemed to me to get lower and lower every minute. Gradually it seemed to die out; but I thought it was my inexperience which imagined it, and I had no fear but that she would revive when she was properly treated. Presently I heard Dr. Murray groping his way up the dark stairs, and for very joy I ran out to meet him.

"What brings *you* here, in this terrible place?" he asked.

"My business," I answered. "Would to heaven I had come sooner! But come in and see this poor woman; the baby is dead, I think," I said, sadly.

"Dead!" he said, looking at it; "still-born."

And laying it down, he looked towards its mother. His face was very grave—I thought a little anxious—as he touched the woman's pulse, then her heart, and finally laid his head upon her chest. "Dead also," he said, sorrowfully, rising from his kneeling posture.

"Then it's my fault"—I was beginning, but I stopped.

There was a shriek behind us, and turning round I found my poor Little Meg fainting on the floor. Dr. Murray quickly restored her, for it was but a momentary swoon, and then I asked him what was to be done.

"Done!" he said, passing his hand across his forehead: "with this poor child you mean?"

"No, with the mother and the baby; I will mind the girl."

"Oh, then, I'll inform the parish authorities; and meantime I'll send a trustworthy woman I know to watch beside the dead."

"Mayn't we wake mother?" said Meg, piteously.

"Wake her, child?" said the doctor; "you can't; she's asleep—forever."

Dr. Murray was a Protestant, and so did not understand our Catholic usages.

"No, Mary," I said; "it will be more prudent not. Come home with me now, and be sure, my child, we will see that your poor mother is cared for."

"Oh, let me stay with her!" she pleaded.

"My poor child, I don't think it would be wise. When this good woman comes whom Dr. Murray has gone in search of you shall come back to Westfield with me. Is there anything here you would like to take with you?" I said, looking round the room questioningly, for to me there seemed nothing transferable.

"This, please," she said, drawing a wooden Rosary and Crucifix from beneath her mother's pillow. And then the thought struck me for the first time, heart-breakingly, heart-rendingly, that this poor creature had died without the consolations of our most holy Faith.

Why, oh, why had Father Haynes not come to see her? and I reproached him bitterly for his neglect, as I called it. I did not know that the dear old priest had given her Holy Viaticum the day before, nor yet that he was at that very moment on his way to see her. But I just missed him. Dr. Murray's woman arrived, and little Meg and I went out at one end of Angel-street just as the good Father was entering the court.

On, on through the muddy street, Meg and I trudged. We did not speak much; for at moments such as these I always think that one is best left alone: words of human consolation would only irritate—at least I think they would me. Besides, I saw that the child wanted to say her Rosary; so I just told her to put her confidence in the good God, who had promised never to leave the orphan, and I said a few words, recommending Mrs. Stephens's soul, as well as the future of her child, to my sweet Mother the Blessed Virgin, and then my thoughts turned to the material wants of the present moment.

"What would Edith say?" I soliloquised, "and, above all, what would mamma think of this freak of mine, as she would be sure to call it;" for I knew that she would have arrived at Westfield against my return, and would be, perhaps, a little hurt at my not being there to receive her, after a separation of more than two months. In the midst of my perplexity a bright idea came to me: surely, I thought, the Blessed Virgin has inspired me with it; and on arriving at home I acted on my "bright idea."

I led Meg into the house through the conservatory, then through the drawingroom, where I knew no one would be at that hour; then up the back stairs, and having safely deposited her in my own little bedroom, I breathed a sigh of infinite relief. "Now, Meg," I said, "you must stay here, like a good child, until I return; I shall not be very long," and quickly taking off my walking things, I smoothed my hair, and went down alone to the diningroom. There, as I expected, I found mamma; and as I entered she came forward with her own sweet smile, and kissed me, just as she had ever done. This reassured me very much; so I determined to go to the charge at once. We were scarcely seated, she in her arm-chair and I on a stool at her feet, when I said: "I suppose you're going to give me a Christmas-box, mamma?"

"Well, certainly," she replied, "that *is* cool. What if I am not?"

"Oh, then, I don't know what I shall do," I said, sadly.

"What's in the wind, *now?*" she said, laughing; for she guessed pretty shrewdly that I had some secret scheme on hand.

"Would you mind telling me what you're going to give me, mamma?" I said, not heeding her question; "and is it already bought?"

"But I never said I *was* going to give you anything, you little witch."

"Oh, mamma," I said, deprecatingly, "*please* don't tease me to-night: it's Christmas Eve."

This remark had the desired effect, and then my mother said more seriously:

"Well, yes, I *am* going to give you a gift—one I think you will like very much too."

"Oh, what is it?" I asked, clasping my hands.

"Guess!"

"I cannot; please, please mamma, tell me."

"What would you say to a horse, then?"

"Oh, mother!" I said, delightedly—for I had been longing for a horse of my own for many years—but my scheme came back to me, and I asked more quietly: "How much is it to cost?"

"When people get gifts," said mamma, "they don't usually inquire the price; but you're a spoiled child, so I suppose I must satisfy you. Well, I entrusted the buying of it to Arthur" (that was my brother-in-law), "and I told him he might give from £100 to £300 for it."

"Oh, mamma," I asked, in suspense, "is it already bought?"

"That I cannot tell, Muriel," she answered, pleased that I took such an interest in it.

"But, mamma," I said, "could you not telegraph to Arthur and tell him I prefer something else, and not to mind the horse?"

Her look changed now from smiling pleasure to keen disappointment.

"But *why* do you wish me to do this, Muriel?" she asked.

"Oh, mother," I said, looking up in her face, with my hands clasped on her knee, "let me tell you my story." And then, in the dim twilight of that Christmas Eve, so many years ago, I told my mother the sad tale of Little Meg and her poor mother. "I wanted to bring her up carefully," I said, "and then to put her in the way of gaining an honest livelihood; but I could not do this without money, and so"—I went on, but not without a suspicious little sob—"and so I was willing to give up my horse if mamma would give me the money instead, so that I might carry out my scheme."

My mother was a truly Christian woman, and I think it pleased her even more to see her child capable of making a sacrifice than to see her pleased with a personal accession; so after a little thought she consented to let me bring up Meg. A telegram was despatched to my brother-in-law, who fortunately had put off purchasing the horse to the New Year. He came home himself that night, and was just beginning to say how sorry he was about it, when I stopped him and told him that he need not mind in the least; but that if he would invest my £300 to the best advantage I should be very much obliged to him. He was a dear good brother, and did not laugh at me, but did just as I asked him; and then, two or three days after, I took Meg myself to a Convent School where I had a cousin a nun. Sister Mary Evangelist received her with motherly kindness; and now and then when I can find time to go and see my little *protegée* I am more than repaid by the bright smiling face for my gracious reception of the " Gift the Christ-Child brought me" so many years ago!

Fourth Night.

MISS SWIPPIE.

Miss Swippie.

PITTER-PATTER, pitter-patter, down came the rain in torrents; and the wind outside was blowing "great guns and little pistols:" blowing as if the playroom windows must at last be stove in, or at least that the trees out in the meadow opposite must be torn up by their roots.

"Naughty little raindrops," said Miss Swippie, tracing with her tiny finger the progress of a drop down the window pane; "*why* can't you stop and let us go out; it's so dull shut up here in the house! They won't let us walk, and they won't let us play, and they won't let us do anything but sit still with our hands before us!"

"For shame, Bob," said her elder brother, using his own peculiar pet name for her, looking up from his fretwork, which he was doing beside the fire; "you *pretend* to love mamma so much, and yet you can't keep quiet, when she's asleep, and when you know she's so ill: why can't you take a book and read like Wilfred?"

"Oh, Wilf can read and *I* can't; I've to spell all the hard words, and it's too much trouble," she answered, going up and giving her little brother a sharp pull of the ear.

"Don't, Swippie," said the little student; "can't you leave me in peace?—you *are* such a tease!"

"All the better for you, my dear," she returned, tormentingly, and beginning to twirl noisily round the room, she accompanied herself by singing a nursery rhyme at the top of her voice.

"Leo, my dear child," said her father, opening the door, and looking at her sorrowfully, "you really must be more quiet. Your mother had just fallen asleep, and now you've awakened her; if you go on in this way, you must really be sent away until she gets better."

"I'm awfully sorry, papa, indeed I am," she began, with an air of contrition; "but it is so frightfully dull, and I've nothing to do!"

"Play with your doll, then," said her father: "surely you've plenty of toys?"

"Yes, but I want to go out; it's so lonely indoors."

"Take a book and read, then," suggested Mr. Hildyard.

"Master Thomas Torment has already told me to do that, but it's too troublesome; I hate spelling the hard words."

Her father sighed, and left the room, without proposing any further amusement; but he was thinking to whom he could send this pet child of his during his wife's dangerous illness; for go she must: the doctor had told him only that morning that Mrs. Hildyard's recovery depended solely on the rest and quiet of the house. So returning to the sick-room he took pen and paper, and wrote a short note, begging two old maiden ladies, who had known and loved his wife in her girlhood, to have the charity to take Leo until the crisis should pass; he added, moreover, that he should send her the next day by the mid-day train; and that if they felt it too great a charge they could send her back again, and he must think of some other person to whom he could entrust her.

Accordingly, next day Miss Swippie was packed off with Master Thomas Torment, as she politely called her elder brother. The Miss

Halls were delighted to see her, and far from sending her back, received her with a depth of love unusual in old ladies for such bothers as children. Tom returned to Mayford that night alone, and Mr. Hildyard's fears for the recovery of his wife were set at rest.

Scarcely six weeks had passed away: spent by Leo in uninterrupted sunshine and petting, spent by her dear mother at home in unceasing suffering and sleeplessness, and by the three other children in a state of mouse-like quietness, which they imposed upon themselves to show their love for her.

It was a bright morning in early April; the February rains had long ago ceased; and if there was a shower now it was a bright, sunshiny one, which only forced Leo to take shelter in the summer-house, but seldom obliged her to stay indoors for long together. The two old ladies were sitting at breakfast, talking about the failure of some Turkish bonds in which they were interested; and Miss Swippie was looking questioningly from one to the other, wondering what "Turkish bonds" meant, and if the poor Turks were always in prison, when turning quickly towards the window she espied Tom coming up the gravel path. He had a black band round his hat and left arm, and his face was pale and sad, but Miss Swippie did not notice that.

"Tom! Tom!" she shrieked, jumping off her high chair. "Lambie," she cried to the younger Miss Hall, "it's Tom;—quick, quick;" and away she flew to meet him.—Poor little child! she really loved her brother, though she was so rude to him; and now as he stooped down to kiss her, she hugged him until he begged for mercy.— "What's this, Tom?" she asked presently, catching at the band on his arm. "Are you going to play 'Sambo,' like the man in the circus?"

"Nothing, Swippie; run up and get on your things, though; papa has sent me to fetch you; we are both going home together."

"How lovely," exclaimed Leo, with more truth than politeness, after all the kindness and care the dear old ladies, who had followed her from the breakfast-table, had shown her. "Do you hear, Lambie? I'm to go home with Tom."

"But why, Tom?" began Miss Hall.

The boy made an imploring gesture in Leo's direction, and told her to make haste and get ready or she would be late for the train. She needed no second bidding, and ran off, leaving her brother to tell the sad news of her mother's death to the Miss Halls.

"Papa told me not to let her know of it, if I could help it, until we were nearly home. He said it was no good frightening her until the time came for her to see mamma," he added.

"Yes, perhaps it is wiser to keep her in ignorance," said Miss Hall, sadly. "Here she comes," she added, as the little figure appeared in her warm jacket and fur hat. "Good-bye, Leo."

"Good-bye, Miss Hall," returned Leo, "and good-bye, my own dear Lambie; I'll soon be back again to see you."

Tears were in the good lady's eyes, as she kissed the child, and said, "God bless you, poor little lamb; God bless and shield you from danger."

And then the two children left the house and walked towards the station. They were very silent just at first; Miss Swippie was busy picking her steps, and Tom was thinking sadly of their great and irreparable loss."

"Look, Tom," said Leo, presently, "I can't get over this puddle; you must lift me over."

The boy took her in his strong arms and carried her across gently, without speaking. They had now arrived in George's-street, where there was a good pavement; so Leo's tongue began to move as quickly as ever.

"You've not told me why you've got this black rag tied round your arm, Tom," she said, "and why you're pulling such a long face. Just look at me: you look so!" And she drew her chubby little face into a mute's grimace.

"Make haste, Swippie dear," said Tom, without answering her question; "we've only three minutes to get down Adelaide-road."

At last they were seated in the train; but Tom did not speak any more than he had done during the sad walk from Miss Hall's house to the station. He was more gentle, Leo thought, as he handed her into the carriage; but the blue eyes were filled with wonder at Tom's face, he so seldom looked grave. They had gone about half-way when Tom thought he had better begin to tell her of the sorrow. He scarcely knew how to begin; for he had never had any news of the kind to break before. He took her on his knee, however, and smoothed the golden curls which hung on her black jacket, and then said softly: "Leo, mother's above us."

"What, Tom," said the child, laughing, "is she on the top of the train?"

"No, darling," he answered, "she's in heaven, and now she's looking down on us, her two children, and she sees everything we do, and she hopes we are very good;—and we will be good, Leo, for her sake, won't we?"

"But Tom, I can't tell what you mean," returned Leo, impatiently; "you say that mother's above us, and that she's not on top of the train, but that she is in heaven. How could she get there, she had no wings?"

"No, my poor little sister, but an angel came down from heaven this morning and bore her away on his wings to be with God forever. Leo, darling, mother is dead!"

There was half a second of bewilderment as if she scarcely understood the words aright, and then the fountain of her tears was loosed, and the little soul broke forth into a piteous wail. She did not know exactly what death meant, but she had a vague idea that it was something very dreadful that had taken her dear mamma away from her so that she would never hear her voice again. For, dear little ones, I have not told you something about poor little Miss Swippie which was very sad. She was not like you, a little Catholic: her parents were Protestants; and if it had not been for the dear old nurse at home, Leo might have grown up as bad as a little heathen, for her mother was always too ill to teach the children anything, and I am afraid their father, good as he was to them, and much as he loved them, cared very little about their souls' salvation.

Tom did his best to soothe the sobbing little creature on his knee, and when the guard came in to collect the tickets, the good man was touched at the sight of her tears.

"What's the matter with the little maid?" he asked, kindly.

"Our mother died this morning," said Tom, "and I've only just told her."

"Poor lamb! poor little lamb!" said the guard. "I wonder would she like this." And he offered her a large orange.

Poor Miss Swippie! Her sorrows were forgotten, and she smiled through her tears as she accepted the fruit, which occupied all her attention until they reached Mayford.

"Let me take her in!" pleaded Tom, as the nursetender took Leo's hand to lead her to her dead mother's bedside.

"No, Master Tom, you could not carry her. Come, Miss Leo." And she lifted her burden tenderly and bore her away.

There was silence in the death-chamber—a silence only broken by the sobbing of Leo's two aunts, who were her mother's sisters. Mrs.

Murphy carried the child to the coffin in which lay Mrs. Hildyard; she had died in great agony, as was apparent by the expression of the mouth, from which Leo turned away frightened.

"Won't you kiss your mamma, Miss Leo?" said Mrs. Murphy.

"Can't," said Leo, shortly. "I don't like the way she looks now."

The nurse did not press her to kiss the dead, but took her quietly back to the nursery; and there Leo began to contemplate the new arrival in the shape of a baby-brother. And sometimes, nay, often and often in after years, until the time when Faith came to point her to her *two* mothers in heaven, she would yearn for and grieve that she had not kissed the cold brow of her dead mother. The funeral ceremonies were over, and they had borne Leo's mamma far away to the home of her childhood, and laid her in the old churchyard by the sea, where the salt waves came twice a day to sing her requiem, and the tall old yews waved mournfully in the evening breeze.

I think Mayford would have continued in its death-like stillness if Miss Swippie had not been there; but as she said herself, "she kept them all alive, as there seemed nobody else to do it." It was very sad to see her in mourning; her bright plaid had suited her so well; but now the deep black made a regular little scarecrow of her. Etta, her elder sister, felt her mother's loss very much, and Miss Irwin, Mrs. Hildyard's maiden-sister, said she really must take her pet down to Cork, where her brother lived, for change of air. So she wrote and told him that they were coming, adding that she would much prefer his coming up to fetch them, as she disliked travelling alone. Accordingly, Uncle George came up, and the day of their departure was not only arranged, but had arrived, and the three travellers were sitting at luncheon before starting, when Miss Swippie bounced into the diningroom.

"Hallo, Leo," said her uncle, "why aren't you coming to Cork? Should not you like to?"

"Shouldn't I, though?" she answered, clasping her hands in a manner quite her own.

"Well, then, away with you and get dressed, and if you're ready in time I'll bring you with me!"

"May I, though?" she said, looking askance at her father.

"Are not two too many to lose at once?" said he, gently.

"Never mind, Thomas," returned his brother-in-law, "you'll have the boys left; you can easily spare me the girls. Away with you, Swippie."

Upstairs ran Leo like an arrow, screaming out: "Nurse, nurse, Uncle George is going to take me to Cork with him; my crape dress and my crape hat—quick, quick, quick! Mary, pack up my things immediately, please."

"What!" gasped Nurse Watkins, "sure and never a word was said about your going. I thought only Miss Etta was?"

"Not until this minute;—but please make haste, nurse!"

The tears sprang to Nurse Watkins' eyes as she got ready her little charge, whom she loved most dearly.

"And who'll hear you your prayers of a night, my poor lamb?" she said, sorrowfully. "Who'll teach you to pray to the Sacred Heart and to love the Blessed Virgin? They'll take you to their meeting-houses like they did last Sunday, and then what'll become of you? Oh, *wirra! wirra!* Mary, have you the clothes packed?"

The nursemaid had been quick; and Leo's wardrobe had been neatly placed in a small portmanteau.

"Thanks, Mary," said the child; "thanks, ever so much, for being so quick. When I come back from Cork, I'll bring you some candy in return for your trouble."

"It's nothing to speak about, Miss Swippie," returned the maid; "and I'd rather you'd say a few *Hail Marys* for me than the candy."

"All right, Mary," said Swippie; "good-bye." And she held up her face to be kissed. "Good-bye, my dear old nurse," she said, going over to the old woman, and stroking her wrinkled cheeks fondly; "never mind, either. I'll *always* love my own Church; and they shan't, and won't, and can't make me love any old place like they took me to last Sunday. And I'll always love the Blessed Virgin, and I'll soon be back with you, dear, dear nursie. Good-bye!"

Mrs. Watkins' caught her troublesome darling to her bosom, and after a long embrace Leo was released, and she ran gaily downstairs to where the carriage was waiting. The journey to Cork was a long and a cold one. Uncle George, Aunt Kate, and Etta slept nearly the whole time; but Miss Swippie did not even close her eyes. She was busy looking at the sky, and, though no astronomer, she had ideas of her own about the heavenly bodies. She imagined that the stars were pin-pricks which God had made in the deep blue of heaven's floor, and their tiny lights were the reflection of the "sea of light" with which the home of the Almighty was flooded. By the time they reached Cork Miss Swippie was tired in spite of herself; the little sand man had been his rounds, and had thrown plenty of bags of dust in *her* eyes; so Cousin Lizzie, Uncle George's only child, took her up to bed and undressed her. But when prayer time came, and Leo, now fully awake, knelt down reverently and began: "In the name of the Father, and of the Son, and of the Holy Ghost. Amen;" and crossed herself, she was struck dumb with horror; and scarcely knowing what the child was saying, except that they were popish prayers, she let her continue. "Five Hail Marys for Mary the nursemaid." Leo always understood by "few" the number "five," and so you see she did not forget her promise to Mary. Then she went on: "O my God, I adore Thee, and I love Thee with all my heart; I believe and hope in thy great goodness. Blessed Virgin Mary, pray for me; my good angel watch over me. Good-night, sweet Jesus; I give you my heart, and I promise always to be very good for the love of thy Sacred Heart. Amen."

By the time Miss Swippie had got thus far, Lizzie had recovered her speech, and she said, sternly: "Who taught you to pray like that, Leo?"

"I learnt it," replied Swippie, shortly.

"Who taught you to pray like that, Leo?" still more sternly.

"I *learnt* it," said Leo, still more shortly; "and what's it to you *who* taught it me, or *where* I learnt it?"

This speech was very rude, and the sweet prayer she had just uttered little justified it; I am sure, also, that it grieved her Guardian Angel very much.

"*I* know who taught it you!" said Lizzie, angrily.

"Then, if you knew, why did you ask me?" inquired Leo, pertly.

"It was that hateful old Mrs. Watkins, I'll be bound."

A word against her dear old "nurse," and Miss Swippie was in arms.

"How dare you say that, Lillie?" she said, angrily. "Nursie's the best, the sweetest, the kindest old woman that ever lived!"

"There, there, be quiet, Leo," said her cousin, hastily, for Miss Swippie was sobbing as though her heart would break. She was a smart child, and she well knew how much her parents disliked Roman Catholics: indeed, it was because they could procure no others that were trustworthy, that they allowed their servants to belong to the despised Faith; and Leo thought, and rightly, that Mrs. Watkins would be sent about her business if her father knew she had taken her to Mass, or taught her Catholic prayers.

The next day was Sunday. Aunt Kate took Etta and Leo to church, as nurse had feared she would. Such a cold, dark place it was, Miss Swippie thought: so different from the chapel at home, where nurse used to take her during her mother's long illness. Most of the people came in quickly and irreverently, and walked straight to their seats; and the child looked in vain for the Tabernacle that she might bow before it. She was sorely disappointed, poor little thing! The high square pews, like horse-boxes, frightened her, and it was not until she was placed against the parapet in the family pew in the gallery that she forgot her trouble, in a measure at least, as she watched the numbers stream in.

Lady Seaton's pew was directly below theirs, and Leo laughed softly to herself at the flower-garden of a bonnet she had on her head. She looked up, evidently to see if Miss Irwin was there, for they had ever been friends; and seeing her, she nodded smilingly, while Aunt Kate as smilingly returned her salutation.

Once more Swippie was troubled. What a queer place it was; what a strange "House of God" (if indeed it were the House of God), as nurse had taught her to call church, if people recognised each other and made visits by signs in it. The tears now filled her eyes; for where was the altar? *She* could only see a square table with a red cloth on it. And where were the lights and the little boys dressed in white? And the beautifully vested priest? *She* could only see two men come out of the vestry in white surplices; one went to the reading desk under the pulpit, while the other went and sat beside the red table and did nothing.

Prayers had begun; the curate was droning out the Litany; it was very, very wearying, Leo thought, and a sudden fit of mischief seized her. Taking a beautifully bound Bible, her godmother's last birthday gift, she quietly took out the first leaf, and tearing it into tiny atoms, she seized a handful and flung it down, as she intended, on Lady Seaton's flower garden; but the aim was unhappy; the paper shower rained instead on her husband, Sir James, who was devoutly saying his prayers to his hymn-book. He looked up to inquire the cause, and Leo shrank back, ashamed of being seen; but Aunt Kate guessed something was wrong, and finding what it was, she lifte Leo from the seat, shook her, and promised her a sound whipping when she got home. But Uncle George shielded her; he was no church-goer himself, and asked his sister what on earth made her expect so young a child to sit through so long and dismal a service? And so Swippie escaped.

A few days after Uncle George proposed a visit to Spike Island. Leo clapped her hands and was delighted; but Aunt Kate said, "No, not to-day; they would go up the river; but she must stop at Queenstown, as she had some visits to pay."

"Then let *us* row out to the Island," said her brother.

"No," returned Aunt Kate, "you must come with me: you at least owe your duty to society, George;" as much as to say he did not owe it to his God also.

"And who will mind the children when we're gone?—for you never will bring them to people's houses with you!"

"Oh, they can stay on the jetty; Leo's so active she'll find plenty to amuse her; and Etta and Lizzie are such good children, they will take care both of themselves and of her."

"All right; be it so," assented Uncle George; and so by eleven o'clock they were steaming up the river.

Oh, what a lovely day it was! Leo loved nature very much, and she loved the sunshine—she and it were very old friends—and the blue sky, and the little birds that perched on the masts of the little boat, and the tiny wavelets that washed its sides. She sat down by the railing and threw her head back to look up at the bright azure sky above: but this move, as the aim last Sunday in church, was an unhappy one, and her best crape hat fell back into the water!

"Oh, Leo!" cried her aunt, "what *have* you done?"

"Nothing," returned Leo.

"Nothing! Do you call it nothing to let your best crape hat fall into the water?—Yes, please," she said to the man who offered to fish it out, "but I expect it's useless; the crape is already ruined. O Leo, what a troublesome, naughty child you are!"

"I'm very sorry, Aunt Kate," she said, timidly; "but the elastic fell out the other day."

"And why could you not have asked me or someone to sew it in again?"

"I forgot," she said, piteously.

Ah, Swippie, "I forgot" is one of the "little foxes that spoil the vines," just as "I can't" is its little brother.

There was no further mishap until they reached Queenstown. Perhaps you are asking yourselves "had she not had enough for one day?" but listen.

"Now, Leo," said Aunt Kate, as they left the steamboat, "let me entreat of you to be a good child while we are away, and not to go too near the edge."

Miss Swippie promised to be as good as she possibly could, and thus reassured, her aunt and uncle left the pier.

"Swippie, there's a darling; don't go so near the edge; you'll surely fall in," cried Etta.

"Oh, no fear," answered the young lady; "I'm only going to sit here and watch if I can see any little fishes;" and she seated herself coolly on the very edge of the pier. She looked from the bright blue sky above to the dark green water beneath, and then again from the water at her feet to the heavens; but the jerks she gave her head were not without danger, and in an unguarded moment, when lowering her eyes, she fell forward, and with a piercing scream she tumbled into the cold deep sea.

Etta and Lizzie heard the scream, and their

cries attracted a group of sailors standing near. Not half a minute had passed since Swippie had fallen, though she, poor child, thought it was half a century, when a strong man threw off his coat and shoes, and jumped in after her. He was a good swimmer, and a brave, kind-hearted man, and so he brought his light burden safely and quickly to land again, not much the worse for her fall, but very much frightened and very wet, and moreover having learnt a good lesson of obedience. After this escapade, as you may suppose, Uncle George did not attempt to defend her, and when Aunt Kate proposed that she should be sent home, he raised no objection, and even offered to take her back himself as "incorrigible."

But sorrow of sorrows! when she arrived at Mayford, Nurse Watkins had left: Lizzie had written to her uncle and told him how Leo said her prayers, and so dear old nursie was gone. But never mind! her prayers and her teachings were not forgotten, and they bore fruit abundantly in after years; for listen, dear little ones: after spending nearly all her girlhood in error and as a Protestant, Miss Swippie became a Catholic, and not only a Catholic, but a Sacred Heart Child; and perhaps you may not believe it, but it's Miss Swippie who is telling you these stories!

Fifth Night.

THE LOSS OF THE "HESPERUS"
AND THE
RESCUE OF THE "ARMISTICE."

The Loss of the "Hesperus."

MY sister and I had just come out of church one bright, cold day in March long ago.

"Come, Gracie," I said, "let's catch up with Mrs. Williams; look at her on before us."

We were smart walkers, so it did not take long to reach the lady in question. She was a widow, and had but one son.

"Good-morning, Mrs. Williams," said Gracie, brightly; "it's a lovely day, isn't it?—so bright: only I wish it weren't quite so cold."

"One must expect to be cold in March," said Mrs. Williams; "but it's bright to-day in more ways than one—at least for me. Do you know Charlie will be home to-night?"

"Will he?" I said, gladly. "Then you'll have

a really happy Easter, Mrs. Williams, won't you?"

"That I shall. I'm all impatience until to-night comes. Oh, my pride and my joy, when shall I see you!" she exclaimed.

Charlie Williams was a midshipman, and a dear old playfellow of my own; that was the reason why *I* was glad he was coming home.

"I expect to see him such a tall, broad, strong fellow," continued his mother. "Two years is a long time; and he was already very big for his age when he left us: don't you remember, Alice?"

"Yes," I replied; "but if he's changed in face and figure I hope he won't be in manners; I don't think I should like him at all if he did not laugh and talk like he used to long ago."

"You're complimentary to his mother," said Mrs. Williams, laughing; "but I'm quite sure you won't be disappointed in him," she added, nodding and smiling.

"Gracie," I said, when we had reached Waterloo-street, "I'm just going up to Mrs. Holmes; I promised I would look in this morning and see how her husband is."

And so I left my sister to go on home with Mrs. Williams, as we all lived on the same terrace, while I went to look after the mother of one of my little poor children.

"Do you know the good news, Miss?" said Mrs. Holmes, dusting a chair with her apron for me.

"Yes," I said; "I've only just heard it, though, from Mrs. Williams: the 'Hesperus' is expected in dock to-night."

"Just so, Miss; at five o'clock. Our boy John sent us a letter last night."

"Ah, that news will help a great deal towards his father's recovery, won't it?" said I.

"Indeed it will, Miss; my husband has not been the same man since the postman came last night! John was ever a good, dutiful son to us, Miss; and we've a clear right to be glad he's coming home again. Two years is a long time, isn't it, Miss Ainsworth?—and as regular as the clock he's sent us the better part of his earnings."

"That is really good of him," I returned; "but was he not promoted a short time ago?"

"Yes, Miss, last Candlemas; he's now officer's servant and under steward."

"That is a good position for one so young," I said;—"but I must be going now. I'm glad your husband's better, Mrs. Holmes; remember, if you want anything to send up to me for it, won't you?"

"Indeed I will, Miss, and thank you kindly. Good-morning, Miss." And leaving the cottage, I sped on my way homeward.

The parlourmaid was not long in opening the door when I got there. She, too, had someone on board the "Hesperus," and last night's post had brought her the news that her father, who was head steward, would be home that Sunday night.

"Ah, Miss Alice, only think," she exclaimed, joyfully, "father will be back to-night. Miss Alice, won't you get leave for me to go down to Mrs. Holmes to meet him, for I know he'll go there with John?"

"Indeed I will, Mary," I said; and passing on up to my stepmother's sittingroom, I obtained the desired permission.

"Papa," I said, as we were finishing luncheon, "I'm just going to Mrs. Heathcote's to congratulate her on the admiral's coming home to-night; may I bring her your best wishes?"

"Indeed you may, my dear," replied my father: "and that reminds me, if *I* should forget, don't you forget to write to Harry next mail; he complained how little you wrote to him in his last letter; and you know, poor fellow, *his* ship won't be home for a long time yet."

"Oh, I'm so sorry, papa; and indeed I'll sit down this evening the first thing after dinner and write him a long epistle," I answered; and then I ran upstairs to get on my walking things.

Mrs. Heathcote lived next door but one to us, so my walk was not a very long one; nevertheless, the rain and sleet which had begun to fall during luncheon now drove so hard in my face that they nearly blinded me; and the cold wind which blew from the sea, pierced even my sealskin jacket. The admiral's wife was standing in the window as I ran up her steps, and seeing me she opened the halldoor herself.

"My dear child," she said, kindly, "what on earth made you come out such a day?"

"I only came to tell you how glad I am the admiral is coming home to-night. I heard the good news both from Mrs. Williams and poor Mrs. Holmes," I answered.

"Oh, thanks," she said. "I had a letter from him last night to say he hoped to cast anchor in the Hamoaze about five o'clock this evening: it's such a long time we've been separated," she added, sadly. "I'm going to try and persuade him to leave the Navy, and stay at home. Won't you come in, Alice, and help to while away the time till he comes?"

"Yes," I replied, "I can stay till half-past three; but then I must be off."

So we seated ourselves comfortably by the cheery blazing fire, and Mrs. Heathcote began to tell me about a voyage she had made long ago with her husband, when they were first married, and when he was only a post-captain.

"But I'll never go with him again," she ended. "I had enough of it that time; and I hope he has had enough of it *now*. What! must you be going?" she added, as I rose and put on my hat.

"I'm afraid so; it's twenty past three, and I must go to church, as there's an afternoon service for the children to-day."

You see I was still a Protestant then.

"Oh, Alice," said Mrs. Heathcote, "you're getting entirely too precise; you're forever going to church, and to mothers' meetings, and all that kind of nonsense; I'm sure you'll end by becoming a Roman Catholic!"

"Never fear," I answered, laughing. "Good-bye; I must be off, or I shall get a scolding from the rector for being late."

And leaving my friend I trotted off through

the storm to the old ivy-grown, century-old parish church.

Ah, me! as I think now of that day in March so long ago, my eyes fill with tears, and my heart with compassion and pity! There were mothers expecting their sons, and daughters their fathers, and wives their husbands, to come home to them that stormy night, and yet not one of them ever came!

Far, far out in the channel the good ship "Hesperus" was ploughing the sea, "cutting the waves in fine style," as the old helmsman said proudly, "and making for home as hard as she could!" At the rate she was going, she would surely be in by the time expected, most likely before it. On the forward deck a group of boys were standing: young middies, whose first voyage this had been. The rain and sleet were driving down upon them, too; but they did not mind it: they were weather-proof after their two years' cruise. They had seen many strange sights, and heard many strange sounds since they last saw Plymouth Breakwater; but much as they loved the sea, they were, one and all, very glad to get home again to their fathers and mothers and brothers and sisters. Each sea-chest contained something for everybody; even the servants, from the old housekeeper down to the stable-boy, were not forgotten; the sailor's memory is a long one, and he had brought foreign wonders for all.

The admiral came among them, just as they were wondering the exact minute when they would weigh anchor. Some declared positively that the storm would keep the good ship back; while others said as positively that she had weathered worse gales than this, and never slackened her speed.

"Well, boys," said the admiral, "you'll be glad to get home to-night, shan't you?"

"I guess so, sir," said a young middy, jumping nearly as high as the bulwarks.

"Take care, Leslie; another such jump, and and I'm afraid *you* would not see Devonport to-night!"

"What time shall we be in, sir, exactly?" said another.

"Well, that I cannot say *exactly*; but I *hope* it will be as I said—five o'clock. See, there is Eddystone; they are beginning to light up!"

"Hurrah for old Eddystone!" shouted the boys. "We're only fourteen miles from Plymouth now. Hip, hip, hip, hurrah!"

Abaft board the scene was nearly the same. The sailors were rejoicing, and "touching their glasses to each other," that but a few hours separated them from their wives and children. John Holmes sat quietly in a corner talking to our housemaid's father.

"You'll come home with me to-night, mate," said the young sailor. "My mother will be expecting you, and Mary'll be down at the old place to meet you for sure!"

"Yes, I'm thinking I'll come along with you; poor lassie, how glad she'll be to see us home again; I wonder if she's happy where she is: she never says a word about it?"

"Oh, never fear," said John; "she'd soon tell you if she weren't!"

In the officers' cabin the rejoicing was just as hearty; the doctor was telling a funny story which had happened when he first began his navy career;—but what was that!

There was a lurch, a creak, and then a tremendous crash! O God! the good old ship had struck on a rock! There was a shouting of orders from the admiral; they were promptly obeyed, but of no avail: the vessel was already beginning to sink. The boats were lowered—but what boat could live in such a sea? Besides, there was no time to man them! So there they stood, not one craven heart among them—a brave, goodly company of men and boys, within sight of home, and yet going down, down, quickly and surely, to a watery grave, never to see that home for which they had been yearning so earnestly and so long!

In five minutes all was over: the good ship "Hesperus" was under water from bow to stern, from maintop mizzen-mast to keel! Some had struggled with the seething waves, and had tried to reach the land, half a mile off, by swimming. But their efforts were unavailing: one and all, from admiral to cabin-boy, had sunk beneath the waves, never to arise until "the sea gives up her dead!"

And, oh! how shall I describe the weeping and the wailing of the widowed and bereaved, when next day the mournful tidings spread far and wide through the land? "It must have been about half-past four when she went down," so the newspapers said, "but nothing further was known, as not one had survived to tell the tale."

And poor Mrs. Williams, and Mrs. Holmes, and Mary, and Mrs. Heathcote! what could we say to comfort and console them? Then, oh, then it was that I felt the emptiness and unsatisfactoriness of Protestantism! Mrs. Townsend, our next neighbour, and a Catholic, went in to see Mrs. Williams; I, too, did my best to comfort the bereaved mother; but "somehow Mrs. Townsend succeeded best: she seemed to *talk* so little, and to *do* so much," said Mrs. Williams, that I began to wonder what there could be in the despised Faith that made it so consoling; and then it was that for the first time I began to ask questions, which were not answered till more than a year afterwards! And so, you see that I knew four whom the loss of the "Hesperus" had deprived of relations; but even in Devonport and Plymouth alone there were tens and twenties who had to mourn in the same way; and then, what sorrow there was throughout England! Some good people got up a subscription for those whose only means of support lay in the lost ones;—but what could money do to comfort them? Who could give them back their dear ones again? May the good and loving Jesus bind up hearts so torn!

* * * * * * * *

The Rescue of the "Armistice."

THE last good-byes had been said, and Mr. Stapleton was hurrying his only son and daughter into a cab, so as to catch the mail which left Westland-row for Kingstown. The night was cold and dark, and the weather seemed to overshadow the bright prospects of any who might be out to seek pleasure. But such was not Harry Stapleton's errand: his was the call of duty! He was a young midshipman, and had just been spending his holidays at home in Ireland; and now on this wet New Year's Eve he was crossing to join his ship at Portsmouth.

"I think you did foolishly, Harry," said his father, "to send your sea-chest on before; you'll have a great deal of bother about it in London, I'm afraid!"

"Oh, no; I don't think so, papa," answered the boy. "I know the guard on the railway, and he will have an eye to it."

"Well, have you all your small traps all right?"

"Yes, sir. Come, Aileen, why are you so silent?" he said to his sister, who was sitting back in the railway carriage, *not* sobbing, as perhaps you may suppose, but looking fixedly at her brother.

"I was only thinking," replied Aileen.

"And of what?"

"Of what I should like you to bring me when you come home again!"

"You greedy little being!" he exclaimed; "so you're not the least bit sorry that I'm going?"

"Oh, yes, I am; only what's the good of crying? it won't keep you back."

"That it certainly won't," said Harry, decidedly;—"but come, now, make known these wants of yours, that I may be able, if possible, to satisfy them."

"Well, I only *want two* things. Of course there are a great many others I should *like*, and which, if your heart is charitable, you will bring me; but I *want* very badly an India worked muslin dress, and an ostrich feather a yard long!"

"You vain little monkey!" said her brother, pinching her ear. "Well, now, I must try and remember. Here we are, though! Come along; let me help you out."

"Take care, Harry, or you'll have me down,"

exclaimed Aileen. "Please, papa, hold me: sailors are always so rough!"

"Thanks for the compliment, Aileen," said Harry, laughing. "But there's the first bell; won't you come aboard until the second rings?"

"No; I'm afraid the boat would start and take me with it; and I don't want to leave Ireland just yet."

"All right, then; good-bye;" and he took her gently in his arms and kissed her. She was sorry to lose him; and now that the parting had actually come, she could not keep the tears back, and whispered with a little sob:

"Good-bye, dear old Harry; I'm sorry I've teased you so often, and been such a bother to you! Good-bye, dear old brother, good-bye!"

Mr. Stapleton then led Aileen back to the train which was waiting to take them to Dublin; and thus on that cold December night, the last of the year, amid torrents of rain, Harry said good-bye to his native land for nearly five years.

And now let us turn to another parting which was, to me, infinitely more touching. It was a widow, whose only son was going out to sea on the same ship with Harry Stapleton. They were seated in a third-class carriage in a train which had left London about twenty minutes ago.

"Willie, boy," said the widow, sadly, breaking the silence for the first time, "you'll think on your poor old mother sometimes, won't you?"

"Oh, mother," he answered, "and how could I forget you?"

"And you'll not forget the good God above us, will you, Willie? I'd rather you'd forget me than Him. There'll be many to scoff at you for saying your prayers and trying to do right; but keep a brave heart, my son, and the Blessed Virgin will help you."

They were silent again, and did not speak until the train stopped at Portsmouth, just opposite the man-of-war to which the boy belonged.

"Farewell, my son," said his mother, through her tears: "I'll leave you now; we could never keep together in such a throng. God protect and bless you, and may his Holy Mother watch over you!"

"Good-bye, mother; don't forget to pray for me on dark and stormy nights!"

She scarcely heard his words, the shouting was so great, and left him before he had done speaking.

And so the two boys went on board: the young midshipman, and the poor little cabin-boy, who in after years became a great admiral. They were only just in time; and then the great engines began to work, and the stately ship moved slowly, slowly out of harbour. She sailed down the Channel that night, and next morning the middies assembled on deck discovered Plymouth before them, with Stratton Heights to the right of them, and Mount Edgecombe on the left. It certainly was a wild, grand scene! There lay the Breakwater, with the curious break-neck steps by which people ascended it; and further on the Hamoaze, with its numberless ships and boats; and over and above all could be heard the wind moaning and whistling with January savageness, and the waves tossing and breaking on the distant shore.

But they were "Outward bound," and in a very short time had said farewell to Old England, for at least four years. Poor little fellows! for some of them it was the first time they had left their native land, and though they loved old Neptune (that is a name sometimes given to the sea) very much, nay, with all their hearts, they could not but feel a little choky to find themselves on that wild waste of waters.

On and on the "Armistice" went; slowly but surely they passed the French coast, through the Bay of Biscay, then by Portugal, and then down along the coast of Africa. They cast anchor somewhere near the Senegal River, and then the middies begged a holiday, and got leave to be rowed, or rather to row themselves ashore, to see the funny natives. And such funny creatures as they were! with great thick lips, and faces as black as ink, and dark rolling eyes. The king of the tribe was very good and friendly to the strangers, and showed them all around. Somehow Harry Stapleton got behind the others, and staying to examine the old chief's cabin, they went back to the boats without him! When he found what had happened to him he was terribly frightened; for the "Armistice" had weighed anchor and was gone far away south.

Harry searched his pockets for something with which to bribe the old chief, and finding a sovereign in one of them, he besought him to send him after his ship. So twelve strong natives manned a long boat, which looked to Harry a great deal too light to live on the sea, whatever it might do on the Senegal; but the chief told him that if he would not go in that, that he might remain where he was; and Harry would not at all have relished that; so he stepped in after the niggers, and with great long pulls with their oars, which sent the little bark skimming over the waters like a bird, they gained on the "Armistice" in about six hours. I need not tell you that the captain punished Master Harry for staying behind, and I don't think he has done such a foolish thing since.

But now comes the exciting part of the story. The vessel was getting very near the equator (which, as you know, is an "imaginary line which runs round the earth, and where there is equal day and night, because the sun always shines directly over it.") They were just a little north of it, when one morning the captain and crew woke up to find themselves "becalmed." Of course the "night-watch" knew of it before, but the middies were very much surprised, and at first very much delighted at the thought of an adventure. But as the day advanced and the sun became hotter and hotter, and the water became not only scarce, but so bad as not to be drinkable, they changed their minds; and when one of the officers told them that they would probably be like that for some days, perhaps even (but he did not tell *them* the "perhaps" as I am telling you) perhaps even they might die of thirst there, unless the wind arose and enabled them to get on their way! the little fellows among them became very frightened, though the big ones pooh-poohed it and remarked sagely that there were "worse misfortunes than that at sea."

The water, as I said, began to fail; and the thirst of everybody on board was almost unbearable. They could not drink the salt water;—indeed there seemed none to drink, though they were surrounded by it. It looked just like a slimy pond, covered with that green stuff which you have heard people call "animalculæ," only the animals here were a great deal larger than any you have seen in ponds! Such horrid monsters they were, and there were nasty smelling plants in the sea like decayed cabbages, and thus it was that the "Armistice" was becalmed, for the wind blew not a breath, and so the good ship could not stir through all that slime.

The third day they were beginning to despair: the captain had ordered that the water should be given out in very little quantities to each person; but with all the care the bursar had taken, he could not prevent it becoming putrid with the intense heat.

Poor little Willie, the widow's son, was

praying hard to the Blessed Virgin that a wind might arise, when his prayer was answered. Who ever called upon Our Blessed Lady in vain?

It was dark night now, yet not so very dark, because the nights down about the equator never are; and the captain was anxiously hoping for a breeze. He stood high up on his own little deck, turning this way and that in his anxiety, when suddenly he thought he felt a light breath on his cheek. Oh, what joy! Yes, indeed, it *was* a breeze, and gradually but surely the wind arose and cleared away the nasty slime in which the "Armistice" had been becalmed. But the troubles of the crew were not at an end. You know their water had all run out, and where could they get more? The salt sea could not slake their thirst. Once more little Willie the cabin-boy asked the Blessed Virgin to come to their help, as she had rescued them from a slow but torturing death. And again our dear Mother heard her child's prayer. The captain was standing on deck consulting with the second officer what was best to be done, when there was a shout from the mast-head, "Ship, ahoy!" The captain drew out his telescope, and there, sure enough, was an English man-of-war—he could tell it by the colour of her flag. Then he hoisted the signal of distress, and the "Warsprite" came to the rescue of her sister-ship. This was the first real danger in which either Harry Stapleton or Willie had been; and you see how Our Lady brought them out of it. May she guard and protect and hear our cries for those in peril on the sea this awful night!

Sixth Night.

UP THE TAMAR IN A STEAM-BOAT, AND DOWN A TIN-MINE IN A BASKET.

Up the Tamar in a Steam-boat,

AND

DOWN A TIN-MINE IN A BASKET.

 AM sure you are laughing at such a funny title; but it's quite true, as you shall see.

It was a bright morning in early July, and Mr. Seymour and his two little daughters were seated at breakfast in a cosy room in their home at Devonport. Such a nice breakfast-room it was; I only wish every little boy and girl had such a cosy one. No, though, on second thoughts, I don't quite think I do; for if that were the case, many little hearts would not have so much to offer to the loving Heart of Jesus, and thus their merit would be lessened. But to our story!

"Papa," said Gertrude, the younger little girl, "I wish you'd take us up the river to-day: it's *so* fine, and you've promised us ever so many times, and ever so long ago!"

"Do you call last week ever so long ago, Gertie?" said her father.

"No; but, papa, really," she said, coaxingly, "there's to be an excursion to-day. I saw it written up yesterday in the town."

"And do you mean *us* to go in those filthy steam-boats that run up and down the river for cheap excursions?" put in Monica Seymour. "*I* thought papa would hire a row-boat and take us that way; but if we're to go in those dirty old things I'll stay at home!"

"Very well, then, *do* stay at home," said Gertie, decidedly, "and papa and I'll go alone; won't we, papa?"

"Oh, nonsense, Gertie, we can't leave Monie at home; but, my child, what is your objection to the steamers? *I* don't see anything wrong with them; they seem to be nice clean little boats; and I know the company have taken great pains to make these excursions both cheap and pleasant for the poor people."

"It's not exactly the boats——" began Monica.

"Well, what then?"

"Oh, it's the people; there are such crowds, and they're so rude and rough."

"Then, if that is all, I will take care of you. Come, run up stairs, and get on your hat and jacket, and ask nurse to put up a few things that each of you might want for a day or two. I received an order this morning from Mr. Winsom, which will let us visit his tin-mines out beyond Calstock, and he has kindly told us to use his little cottage for as many days as we like, so that we may see them thoroughly: I only mean to stay till to-morrow evening, though; so run off the pair of you and get ready in a trice."

It was a wonder that Gertie let her father say so much without interrupting him; but she did: her wonder got the better of her joy; but her tongue-strings loosened as she was being made ready, and, oh! *I* dare not try to describe her gladness. A ride up the river in a steam-boat! a visit to a tin-mine! and then a ride home again, on the river, in the market-boat! *She* at least did not mind whether the steamer was dirty or clean, or how many people were on it, nor how rude they were! When they arrived at the jetty, they had a little time to wait; for as it was an excursion boat, it had to put in at a good many more places than the ordinary market-boat did. At last it arrived, however, and Mr. Seymour, Monica, and Gertrude stepped on board.

I wonder if any of my little readers have ever seen the Tamar! If not, I must try and describe it to you. Of course you know that three towns are built at its mouth: Plymouth, which is a very large place; then Stonehouse, which is smaller; and then Devonport, which is only just beginning to grow up. Far out, about three miles away in the sea, you see the grand old Breakwater, which by-the-by, is almost as great a favourite with the holiday people as the Tamar itself. Then on your right hand you see Mount Edgecombe, and the Hall, which belongs to the earl. I remember seeing from my bedroom window in Devonport what looked to me like a large stork standing in her nest, right up at the tip-top of the hill, but which in reality was only a queerly-shaped tree, as I found out when my brother took me up Mount Edgecombe for a day's pleasure.

But where Monica and Gertrude Seymour started was just below the immense dockyard, and they could hear the great hammers working to and fro, and the voices of the men in the yard as they repaired the Queen's big ships. Presently the little excursion-boat began to move. Gertie thought it was delightful, and Monica pronounced it to be not so bad after all; "if there were only a first-class place reserved she could not complain of it."

"You silly little girl," exclaimed her father; "who ever put these hoity-toity notions into your head? To hear you speak one would think you had at least the weight of three kingdoms on your head, instead of being plain little Monica Seymour!"

"But, papa, really it's not very pleasant to be mixed up so with these rough people—now is it?'"

"We are all equal before God, Monie," said her little sister, gravely. "Maybe some of these poor people you are running down so may be as bright as gold before Him—their souls, I mean—and maybe——" but here she stopped.

"And maybe?" asked Monica.

"Oh, it doesn't matter," said the child, turning away her face, so that Monica could not see its wet eyes. It pained the loving little heart to hear her sister talk so unkindly of poor people.

"Oh, but it does matter. Now, tell me what you were going to say?"

"Well, then, I thought perhaps that people like us, with plenty of clothes to wear and plenty to eat and drink, might often offend God by talking so against the poor. Oh! look there, papa; what place is that?" she added, pointing to a large bridge.

"That is Saltash Suspension Bridge. Some day we'll drive out and see it. The train passes over it many times every day; it cannot get into Cornwall, at least at the south, but by going over it."

"And, papa, just do look at that man hallooing to our steamboat; surely they won't stop for him?"

"Oh, but they will; that poor woman he is rowing out wants to get her day's pleasure as well as anyone else. Would you like to stay here, Monica, while Gertie and I go round the boat and see what's to be seen; we are going among the very poor people, and you may prefer remaining here?"

But being left alone did not at all suit Miss Monica's fancy; so she got up, and holding one hand of Mr. Seymour, while Gertie clasped the other, they moved towards the stern of the boat.

"How long do you think we shall be before we reach Calstock, captain?" asked their father of the skipper.

"We'll make for it in about an hour and a half, sir, I think.

"Are you going any farther then?"

"Yes, one station more, where we'll put up till this evening, and then at seven o'clock I'll be back at Calstock to take up the passengers. Will you be with us, sir?"

"No; I shan't be returning till the day after to-morrow: my little daughter was anxious to go up the river on a steamboat, and so I'm taking them both to see Mr. Winsome's mine out beyond Calstock Hill."

"It's grand weather for a trip like that, sir."

"Yes, I hope it will keep fair for those poor people; they seem to be enjoying their outing so much!"

That indeed they were. A German band had been engaged for the day, and some of the holiday seekers had begun to dance to its lively strains; but the children had now reached the end of the boat, and Gertie was more taken up with the lovely scenery around her than with the people on board.

"Papa," she said, "what's that great big ship for?"

"It's to make naughty little boys good men, Gertie!"

"But how, papa; surely that big thing can't make them better?"

"No, that big thing, as you call it, cannot of itself make them good; but *living* on the big thing can, or at least it is hoped it will."

"But how very still it looks!" said Monica. "Why aren't the little boys running about on it?"

"That's just it," answered her father; "they are kept very strictly there, and have a great many things that they *must* do, and a great many rules which they *must* remember, or else they will be punished: and you know they would not like that, would they?"

"I suppose not," said Gertie, thoughtfully; "but still I think it's very unkind of people to punish poor little boys."

"But if they have done wrong, Gertie, what then? Must they not be taught better?"

"I suppose so," returned the child; "but all the same, I'm very sorry for them having to live on that horrid old thing: it must be very lonely for them."

"Not half as lonely as you imagine," said her father; "and numbers of the boys are very sorry to go when they must leave it."

"What a beautiful place that is, papa," said

Monica. "Just look at the swans, and the dear little boathouse; to whom does it belong?"

"I really don't know, dear; but it is evidently some gentleman's country-seat; see how wide the river is just here!"

Just then a poor old woman came up with a basket, saying: "Any nice muscles to-day, sir, or cockles fresh caught this morning?"

"What disgusting things!" exclaimed Monica, disdainfully. "How on earth can people eat them?"

"With a pin-point," readily answered the old woman, misunderstanding the little girl's meaning; "and the people finds 'em very good, they do, and mighty cheap: only a penny for this lot," and she presented a small saucerful to Monica.

"No, thanks," said Monica, turning away; "not any for me."

"Here, then, old woman, I'll have some," cried Gertie.

"Oh, Gertie, how can you? said her sister, reproachfully; "they will surely make you sick!"

Nevertheless, Gertrude did take some of the cockles, and said she thought them very good. Then they strolled down to the stern of the boat, and Mr. Seymour had a chat with the old helmsman, while the two children amused themselves watching the beautiful banks of the Tamar.

"Papa," said Gertie, "do just look at that house perched on the rock, right above the river; why, if anyone were to fall out of one of the windows they would be drowned."

"That's Cotehele Castle, Gertie," said her father, "and it belongs to a Colonel Somebody, who is Master of the Mutleigh Hounds."

"It's a lovely place," said Monica: "just such a place as I should like to live at, and not at stuffy old Devonport!"

"Oh, for shame, Monie! How can you cry down the dear town so? you've told me times out of mind how much you loved Devonport!"

"But that isn't to say that I could not love some places far better, is it?"

"Well, I suppose not; anyhow, I think I'd say what I mean, and not be praising a place up to the skies one day, and another calling it stuffy and old!"

"Oh, you're such a little saint, Gertie, I've no patience with you," put in Monica.

"A saint! indeed I wish I were. Papa, just hear what Monica says, that I'm a saint; how lovely!"

"Here we are, children," said Mr. Seymour;

"but we must wait until the crowd has passed before leaving the boat, because I must engage a trap to take us up to the mines, and the innkeeper would not have time to pay attention to me, if I asked him in this flurry."

So Gertrude and Monica waited patiently for about ten minutes, and then they climbed up the steep path which led from the river bank to the hotel. There Mr. Seymour easily got a trap, and soon they were fairly on their way to Calstock Hill. First the pony had to go up such a steep hill! Poor little Gertie was terrified lest the horse should slip and send the trap and those in it rolling down to the bottom; then their way lay through lovely country lanes, where the air was laden with the scent of thousands of wild flowers, and where the birds sang in the hedges, and the sky looked deep deep blue overhead. On, on, trit-trot, trit-trot, for five long miles they travelled, and in about an hour they stopped before a gate, above which was written, or rather printed, in large letters, "NO ADMITTANCE EXCEPT ON BUSINESS;" and beyond the gate it looked bare and desolate, until their glance fell upon, oh, such a queer little cottage!

"Why, papa, what's that immense chimney for?" asked Monica.

"I forgot to tell you, children," was the answer, "that Mr. Winsom has brickworks, also; so we shall have a double pleasure: this afternoon we will go over the works, and to-morrow we will do the tin-mine; but first we must get some lunch. I hope the good woman in charge of the house will be able to give us some."

But the "good woman" had not been warned, and so had only her own fare of Cornish pastry and bread and cheese to offer them: but the children thought it romantic, and were quite delighted with it.

"You know, sir," apologised Mrs. Veal, "you know if I'd only know'd ye was comin', I'd have roasted a nice foal for ye!"

There was a titter from the children, and as soon as she had left the room, Gertie exclaimed:

"But, papa, we could never have eaten a whole foal, could we? A foal is a little horse, isn't it?"

"Oh, it's the Cornish dialect, Gertie: she meant a fowl!"

"Then I'm just as glad she didn't, because I like this rough fare very much; don't you, Monie?"

Monica gave a rather doubtful assent. And the meal being over they rose and followed their father out of doors.

"This is the shed where they make the bricks, evidently," said Mr. Seymour. "What a pity that the works are not going: it would be so interesting to watch the processes!"

"But why aren't they going, papa?" asked Gertie.

"All these things take a great deal of money, dear; and Mr. Winsome cannot afford to keep them up."

But Gertie scarcely heard her father's explanation: she was busy playing hide and seek in and out among the rafters of the long, low shed. When they were tired they passed on to the next, which was the drying-shed. Here the roof was very high, and the place quite empty, saving a large pile of ready-made bricks at the door.

"But papa," said Monica, "these bricks don't look like those they build houses with, do they?"

"No, dear, because these are fire-bricks, and are much more expensive than stock bricks, which are used in building. Come now, let us see the engine!"

"Oh, papa, what a monster!" exclaimed Gertie.

"Dear me, dear me!" said Mr. Seymour, as if to himself. "What a pity it is lying idle! I cannot think why Winsome doesn't get up a company for it!"

Monica and Gertrude played in and out among the silent, rust-covered pieces of the great locomotive until they were heartily tired, and said they didn't care to go any further that day, or else they'd not be able to go over the mine tomorrow: they went back to the cottage, and had tea, and then Mrs. Veal put them to bed, while Mr. Seymour examined all the apparatus of the fire-brick factory.

Next morning the children were up with the lark; the sweet air of the Cornish hill woke them up much earlier than they were accustomed to rise in Devonport, and as soon as they were dressed they lost no time in awakening their father and hurrying him over his breakfast.

That over, they ran down the hill before him, pausing for breath at the bottom, until he came up to them.

"It's so delightful, papa, to run about in this wild place," cried Gerty; "I can never romp as I like in the Terrace Garden!"

"And why, Gertie?" said her father.

"Oh, Monie's always teasing about the proprieties; as if there *were* any such things for little girls like me."

"Yes, Gertie, there are proprieties for even such a little girl as you : only I hope you play as much as you want in the garden, do you?"

"Oh, yes, as much as I want, only Monie won't let me climb the trees and run races with the Hope boys!"

"I think she's very right there."

"Do you, papa, really?"

"Yes, really!"

"What are you two talking about so earnestly?" said Monica, coming from the other side of the road, where she had been picking wild flowers for her collection.

"Oh, never mind!" exclaimed Gertie. "See, papa, there is the house belonging to the mine, isn't it? Come, Monie, let's have a race to it!"

So the two set off together ; at the gate they waited for Mr. Seymour, however, not knowing what to say if anyone should open it for them. But before their father arrived, a man came out of the yard, and seeing them, asked, civilly, what "he could do for them?"

"Papa will be here presently, thank you," said Monica, timidly, "and we're only waiting for him."

They had not long to wait : in two minutes Mr. Seymour came up, and telling the man his errand, and mentioning Mr. Winsome's name, they were immediately let into the mine yard. There Monica and Gertrude made acquaintance with the miner's children, whom they expected to see black as little niggers, but who were really healthy, blooming little creatures.

"How long shall we be in the mine, papa?" asked Monica. She began to be frightened rather, when she saw the great shaft and panier in which she was to go down.

"As long as you like, dear," returned her father. "If you wish I'll leave you down there altogether. Many of the miners and their families never come up out of it."

"Oh, no, papa," she exclaimed, shrinking back. "I think I'd rather not go down at all," she added, hesitatingly.

"What!" cried Gertie, amazed; "when papa's brought us from Devonport to do nothing else!"

"Papa, *please* don't ask me to go down; indeed, I'd much rather not," pleaded Monica.

"Very well, my child," said her father, gently. "I would not force you to do anything, much less to do a thing I thought would give you pleasure against your will. Gertie and I will go over the mine together; and you shall stay up here and play with these nice little children, will you?"

Monica thought *anything* would be better than going into that dark, deep hole; and so she consented to stay with the children, though as a rule she preferred grown-up people.

"Now, Gertie, you must go down alone," said Mr. Seymour; "you know the bucket is too narrow to allow of us both going together. Hold tight to this handle, and you'll go down steadily as a queen!"

Gertie grasped the handle at the side of the bucket with all her might, and then the miner began slowly to unloose the ropes which held it at the top of the shaft.

Presently the bucket began to go down, down, down into darkness, deep and terrible. Gertie wondered why they had not given her a light before starting; but she was a brave little girl, and comforted herself with the thought that they must have forgotten it. She was beginning to be a little nervous, imagining they would leave her there perhaps hanging midway between the bottom of the mine and the top, when suddenly she felt the basket alight on something, and a man said, in a gruff voice:

"What's kept ye so long, Jim? We've been awaiting for ye this twenty minutes and more!"

Poor little Gertie did not know what to say to

this; however she stood upright in the basket to let herself be seen, without saying anything. Receiving no answer to his question, the miner looked in the direction of the shaft, and said, as though he did not know what to make of it:

"An' what brings you here, young 'un, if it be'ant impudent to ask?"

"I thought you knew I was coming down," said the child, in a frightened voice. She was so dazzled with the dim light of the man's lantern after the profound darkness of the shaft, that she covered her eyes with her hands. Another man came up now, and asking the matter, he said, kindly:

"Oh, I know all about it; there's a genelman a-comin' down the day, and his two little daters, and so this bese one on 'em likely: come, missy!" And he lifted her gently out of the basket, and then shouted in a thundering voice to the top the words: "Draw up."

Once on the firm ground again, Gertie began to look round her; she was puzzled, and, I think, not a little disappointed; but she was too timid of these great big men to ask them anything; though they did all they could to make her comfortable; and so she waited patiently until her father should arrive.

She had not long to wait, however; and soon, to her relief, she heard the basket coming down the shaft once more. "Oh, papa," she cried, "I'm so glad you've come!"

"Why, Gertie, were you frightened?"

"Yes, just a very little," she replied; "it's so dark; but make haste, papa, and come along: I'm longing to see the bright, shining tin-mine; shall we soon be there?"

"Why, we are *in* the tin-mine, Gertie; what did you expect to see?"

"Oh, papa, you're only joking," she said, reproachfully. "Why, of course the walls must be bright and shining like the tin pans and kettles at Boodle's in Devonport."

"I'm afraid, my poor little woman," answered her father, "if you expected to see such wonders that you will be disappointed. This is the tin-mine; and if we were to go to its furthest end, we should see nothing but these rocky walls, and this mud floor: but if you like, to make up for your disappointment, I will tell you something about tin."

"Oh, yes, please," she said; "only I *did* think we should have seen bright shining walls!"

"Perhaps I ought to have warned you before we came down," said Mr. Seymour; "but really

I never thought you could have had such a foolish idea!"

"Well, but, papa, how was I to know?" cried Gertie. "I'm only eight years old, and I've not learnt about tin yet!"

"Then I will tell you. First of all, you know that it is a metal, a beautiful silvery white metal, with a tinge of yellowish blue, and, as you call it, very bright and shining; but this only comes to it after it has passed through the hands of many, many people."

"Papa, what makes the tin creak when it's bent?" said Gertie.

"I was just going to tell you that: it is because it has crystal in it. You know what crystal is, don't you?"

"Oh, yes, a bright, glassy stone, just like Aunt Edith wore last Christmas when she dressed up as "Winter" to go to the party."

"I really can't say I remember what Aunt Edith wore; but you are right about the crystal. Well, then, the Germans call it the tin-shriek, and the miners down here call it the cry of tin. Tin is a soft metal; you know you can bend it, while you could scarcely even move iron, or lead, or gold; and it can be beaten out into sheets thinner than your nail, and it is then called tinfoil."

"Oh, how wonderful," cried Gertie, who was listening attentively to every word her father was saying.

"Sometimes even they make wire of tin, but it is not very strong, and so breaks easily."

"But, papa, what makes one's hands smell so after one has been touching tin? You know those doll's pie-dishes you gave me my last birthday; well, they *were* so nasty until cook washed them for me."

"I really don't know why it made your hands smell, Gertie, but I believe it generally does; perhaps when I go home I may be able to tell you by looking it out in some book. However, to go on with our object lesson. But first, are you tired? Look here, we can sit down on this stone for awhile, and put the lantern on the ground.

"Oh, how nice, papa! How I wish Monica were here! I'm sure she'll be quite sorry when I tell her all about it. But please go on; I like it so much."

"Well, then, tin is found mostly in Cornwall; there are a few mines in Spain and Portugal, those countries quite at the south of Europe."

"Oh, yes, I know; Madrid is the capital of Spain, and Lisbon of Portugal."

"Just so! Then there are a few more mines in Bohemia, to the south of Germany; and tin is also brought from Australia and Asia. In the early times, long, long before our Lord was born, England was famous for her tin; that and her oysters were the things for which she was first famous; now you know our dear England is famous for lots and lots of other things."

"Yes, iron, and cutlery, and wool, and cotton, and heaps and heaps of things," said Gertie, not being able to remember her last geography lesson on the exports of England.

"As you can see," continued Mr. Seymour, raising the lantern from the ground, so that Gertie might see the walls of the mine, "there is nothing remarkable in tin-ore. You see those great granite and slate rocks; well, it is found chiefly running in veins through these. There are two kinds of tin; that taken from these rocks is called mine-tin; and then there is another kind called stream-tin. And now that we know *where* the tin comes from, we come to a very nice part—that of making it 'bright and shining.' It is very difficult to do this, and takes great care and patience. It is in so many different parts of the rock that it has to be stamped to a very fine powder to separate the tin from the stone. Then this powder is mixed with a great deal of water, which carries it into a channel where there are two pits. The best part of the tin falls into the first pit, and is called the crop; while the remainder, called the leavings, passes through the first and stays in the second pit. Are you tired?"

"Oh, no, not a bit, papa; do go on."

"Well, now, the tin has to be washed ever so many times to take away all the bad parts which might by accident have clung to it. Then it has to be baked in a furnace, to separate from it two other very useful things, about which I may tell you another time, that is, sulphur and arsenic. After this the tin is ready for smelting in another furnace; it is mixed with a little charcoal and lime, but before being put into the furnace it is moistened with water to prevent the powder being carried away by the draught. It is left in the furnace for about six hours, and then the door is opened, and it is stirred round and round to separate the slag, which is raked off and the richer part melted over again."

"But, papa, musn't the poor man that opens the furnace door burn his fingers sometimes?"

"Oh, he takes good care not to do that, Gertie; he knows his trade better than to burn his fingers. Then, when the tin is quite melted, it is poured into an iron pan, from which it is ladled into moulds to make it into nice tidy blocks."

" And is that all ?" said Gertie, rather tired.

"Not quite; there's just a little more; the tin has still to be purified, and this is done by heating it until it runs like water into a basin called a refining-basin, leaving on the hearth of the furnace the bad parts still remaining. Then it has to be poled; and this is done by stirring it with greenwood, which makes a scum rise to the top, which is easily taken away, while the bad parts fall to the bottom, so that the rich and good tin remains in the middle. And now, Gertie, you know all about tin : and not only that, but you've been down in a tin-mine !"

"Yes, papa, I've liked it ever so much; I should like to go down a salt-mine next."

" How do you know that there are such things as salt-mines ?" said her father, lifting her into the basket to go up the shaft.

" Oh, I learnt it the other day in the 'Child's Guide;' there's one salt-mine somewhere in Germany where there's quite a little town ; and the people never come up out of it. Isn't it wonderful, papa ?"

" Indeed it is: now, one, two, three, and away; I shall be up after you very soon !"

And once more poor little Gertie was alone in the basket, but this time coming up out of the mine, instead of going down.

"O Monica!" she exclaimed, when she reached the top of the shaft, "what a treat you've missed!"

"Why, what was it like?" asked her sister, rather sorry she had not gone down also.

"Oh, ever so nice! Papa's been telling me all about tin; the mine itself wasn't very nice, though: not a bit bright and shining like I expected, but all pitch dark."

"But what a little goose you were, Gertie, to expect it to be bright and shining! Why, *I* could have told you that it was nothing but a dirty, dark hole under ground."

"Could you, now?" said Gertie, wondering at Monica's cleverness. "Here's papa," she cried, as she saw Mr. Seymour getting out of the basket. "Oh, what a dear good papa you are to show me the tin-mine! I mean to tell Monica all about it when we get home."

"That's right," said her father; "but now we must make haste back to the cottage and to dinner, and then you two can spend the rest of the day in exploring the place for wild flowers.

But first let us go and thank Mr. ———, the foreman, for his kindness."

"Papa, when are we going back to Devonport?" asked Monica, when they had fairly left the tin-mine.

"To-morrow morning, dear; we'll go down in the market-boat. Oh, what fun!"

"Oh, how nasty!" exclaimed the two children together.

"Yes, Gertie," said Mr. Seymour, "I call it great fun: you'll have to get up at four o'clock in the morning, and walk down Calstock Hill to the boat. Do you think you shall be able to manage it?"

"Why, yes, of course, papa," she answered.

"But why can't we ride?" said Monica.

"Simply because there are no cabs to be had up here."

"But where's the trap that brought us up to the cottage?"

"I quite forgot to tell the man to come back for us; and even if I had remembered it, I don't think I should have ordered it; a walk in the early morning is so nice; don't you think so, Monica?"

"Yes, I suppose so," answered the little girl, doubtfully, and then she ran on to join Gertie, who was busy gathering wild strawberries in the hedges.

Next morning the sun rose brightly, and soon after four o'clock Mr. Seymour and his two little daughters left the hill-side cottage, and wound their way through lovely lanes, where the dew still lay on the flowers, which sent forth their sweet scents. At last they arrived at the water's edge, but no market-boat had yet arrived. A great crowd of people were waiting for it; and nearly everybody to-day had quantities of strawberries to bring to Devonport. It was a great trial to their patience to be kept so long, for the boat was more than half an hour late; however, they made a virtue of necessity, and at last were rewarded by seeing it come slowly sailing down the river. Mr. Seymour and the two children then got on board, and when all the people had safely conveyed their goods on the boat, she continued her journey down the Tamar. Monica and Gertie were very tired after their long walk, and so they chose to remain in the cabin, while their father walked overhead on deck. When they heard the cry "Millbay," they both started up to run to Mr. Seymour, whom they met on the stairs coming to fetch them.

"Well, Gertie, how did you like your

trip?" said he, when they were on their way home.

"Oh, ever, ever so much, papa," she cried, "and when I grow up and am a big woman I shall write a story all about how I went 'up the Tamar in a steam-boat, and down a tin-mine in a basket!'"

Seventh Night.

VOICES FROM THE WEST.

Voices from the West.

WOULD you like to hear how we, children, spent our holidays one long vacation? I will tell you, then.

Our family was rather a strange one—I mean we were strangely related, at least as far as the girls went: the boys were "Auntie's own." First there were Irena and Maude, daughters of a first cousin of "Auntie," and then there was myself, a very, very distant cousin of Uncle Ralph, her husband: but then, she had been my godmother on my conversion to the True Faith; so that I am sure she loved me, if only on that account, while I—but need I tell you how much I loved her!

We three girls—Irena, and Maude, and I—were at school in the Paris Convent: at least

Irena was not at the time of which I speak; she had gone home ill the March before; so Maude and I were left alone; and the boys Willie and Ted were with the Jesuits at Beaumont. One day—it was the anniversary of the Taking of the Bastile, the 14th of July, I believe: no, I remember now, it was the day after, and all the different *Cours* of English, Italian, painting, and the like, were pouring in from the class-rooms to Ste. Madeleine, the great study-hall. Maude was *inspectrice*, but I did not know that; and so when the good sister presented me with a visiting card which bore Uncle Ralph's name, I did not know where to look for her. At first I would not believe that he had come, for we had heard from home only two days before, and they had never mentioned his coming; but when Sister Jones assured me that he was in St. Theresa's, I flew about like a madcap calling for Maude. At last I found her ladyship in the high chair, marking all who were causing disorder in the "*rangement*."

"Maude, Maude," I said, impatiently, "what are you thinking of? Here I've been flying all over the place for you for the last ten minutes, and there you are perched in the chair as cool as a cucumber."

"But what's the matter, Mary?" she said, quietly.

"Why, of course, Uncle Ralph's here; come along quickly, and take off your apron, and put on your gloves!" I commanded.

When we reached St. Theresa's, of course I ran to Uncle Ralph, and hugged and kissed him with all my might; but I had not noticed that he had another gentleman with him; and when I had released him, I heard this friend say: "Which is which, Ralph?"

Now, I forgot to tell you what may seem a very strange thing to you, as it has seemed to many other people much older than you. But Irena had not seen her father since she was a little baby, two years old, and Maude had never seen him at all: for when first he married he brought his young wife out to America, but the climate did not agree with her, and so she came home to Ireland with little Irena, leaving Captain O'Hara still in New York. She had not been long in her native land when Maude was born, and then the mother died, and the two little orphans came to auntie to be brought up. On this 15th of July, then, we could not make out *who* this strange gentleman could be; until Uncle Ralph's answer to his question, "Which is which?" showed us plainly that it was Maude's father. I cannot describe that meeting for the first time, it was so painfully long. Uncle Ralph and I stood by the window talking nervously, with our backs turned on Captain O'Hara and Maude. Presently, however, they came over to where we were standing, and then somehow we got comfortably seated on the sofa, Uncle Ralph and I, while Maude and her father took chairs opposite us.

The Captain proposed to take us out, and Rev. Mother very kindly gave us leave to go: so we went to see "Napoleon's Tomb" and the "Panorama," and after that there was no more time except to go to the Palais Royal for ices, as the train in which Uncle Ralph and the Captain were going on to Vichy started at 7 o'clock, and it was now 5; and they had to dine and drive a long way to the station in those short two hours! We bid them good-bye, and I'm afraid not without tears; but dear good Uncle Ralph cheered us, saying: "Never mind, children, you'll soon be going home; it's not more than a fortnight now to the holidays!" And then they left us, and we forgot our little sorrow in the excitement of the examinations.

A few days after I heard from my uncle; his

hand was very much swollen with gout, he said, but that he must write a line to ask me if I knew anything about the shooting at a place called Fairlawn, about seven miles from Westport, in the county Mayo. I had spent a little time down there long ago—not at that particular place, but very near to it—and so I suppose he thought I might have heard something about the sport. I wrote back to say that I knew nothing of the place, had never even heard the name before, and so *I* could not help him; and we children heard no more about the shooting lodge until we came home three weeks later.

As Uncle Ralph had said, the time *did* pass very quickly, and we could scarcely believe it when the Grand Prize Day dawned, and we were all seated in Ste. Madeleine, dressed in our white uniforms and Congregation medals, and waiting for the cardinal to give us our ribbons. The prizes, however, had been awarded. Maude had gone up for the second medallion, and I for a lower blue ribbon; and so we had spent the rest of the day buying presents for everyone at home. Of course we slept very little that night, and were up the next morning at four o'clock, though we need not have risen until half-past five. All day we travelled to London; and there at Victoria

Station were Auntie and Irena waiting to take us on to Ireland.

All night long, then, we had the unpleasant treat of being in the train, and on the Irish sea; and you may guess how glad I was to hear the stewardess say to a lady, "Yes, ma'am, land has been sighted ten minutes ago!" I crawled down from my berth, and then went feebly on deck to catch the first glimpse of dear old Ireland, as we entered Dublin Bay; but the wind blew my skirts about so, and so nearly took my hat away altogether, that I was obliged to come down again to the cabin.

Willie and Ted were at Westland-row to meet us, and after the due amount of huggings and kissings between schoolboys and schoolgirls —pleasant, perhaps, for these, but I don't think very agreeable for those—we were divided into two parties by Auntie, who put the boys into one cab with Irena and Maude, while she herself got into another with me and most of the luggage. Whether she had dreamed that she had told the boys to drive to Broadstone, or whether she had really done so, I cannot say; but certain it is that when we arrived there there was neither sight nor light of them.

"Oh, they'll turn up by the time we've been

down to Dominick-street to hear Mass; it's the First Friday, you know, Molly, and we must not miss Holy Communion, if we can help it!"

So we went to Dominick-street church; but to our intense disappointment there was to be no Mass until a quarter to eleven; and I had been so careful to take nothing on the journey, that I might have the joy of Holy Communion in the morning! But it was God's will, and so auntie, who was afraid to keep me fasting too long, brought me back to Broadstone for breakfast. But still the boys and girls had not appeared! "What on earth could have happened to them?" said Auntie, rather nervously.

Directly we had done breakfast she called a cab, and we started on a search for them; we went to every place we thought they would be likely to drive to—to Forest's, to Mitchell's, to the hotel at which we generally stayed in town— but nowhere were they to be found. At the hotel the porter told us that "the young gentlemen had been there about an hour and a half before looking for *us:*" and this set auntie rather more at rest; so she went about shopping a good deal, and then in the afternoon we drove back to Broadstone to find Maude, and Willie, and Ted promenading up and down the platform, not dreaming of the anxiety they had given Auntie.

They protested that she had driven off from Westland-row without telling them where to go to, and that acting according to their own discretion, they had gone to the hotel for breakfast, and then had done a little shopping and sight-seeing on their own account.

"Irena went home with a headache in the one o'clock train," ended Willie, "and so we waited here for you, mother!"

I am sure Auntie was very grateful to them for their consideration in waiting for her: only I think she would have been still more so if they had not led her that long dance in the early part of the morning.

When we got home it was raining, and James, the coachman, had brought the waggonette to meet us, as it was very fine when he started; so then we had to huddle together under one big umbrella, and Auntie's and Maude's parasols. There was a letter from Uncle Ralph waiting for Auntie, too, and in it he told her to get everything ready for the West, as he expected to be home next week with the Captain, and that then we were to start for Fairlawn, as he had arranged to take the shooting for the season. This news threw us children into great excitement: I think Willie and Ted wanted to pack up and be off at once, while we girls were nearly as bad, and I proposed that we should not unpack our trunks when they arrived from the station; they would do to go on to Fairlawn as they were!

As Uncle Ralph had said, he and the Captain came home on the 16th of August; and then the preparations began in real earnest. The 20th—the day on which we were to start for the seaside—came at last, and there we were bowling along the dusty roads to meet the early train from Dublin.

William the butler and Mrs. Fowler the cook were driving on an outside car a little before us, and Mrs. Fowler, who was very stout, was swaying to and fro in a most uncomfortable style. At last I could restrain myself no longer, and I burst out laughing.

"What's the matter, Mollie?" said auntie, not at all surprised, for my sudden fits of laughter were known to everybody.

"Oh, auntie," I cried, "do just look at Mrs. Fowler: she'll surely be off the car!"

"Nonsense, child," said auntie, smiling in her turn; "Mrs. Fowler knows how to sit on an outside car as well as you do!"

"Then if she knows no better than I she *will* surely be off; for if I swayed about in that way, no powers on earth could save me from falling," I said.

The car was going over the railway-tracks now, and giving great jerks, at every one of which Mrs. Fowler gave a groan. As it happened, too, I was right about her falling off; it was a great mercy it was not while the machine was moving, but just as she tried to get down she missed her footing, and if Peter the stable-boy had not been there to catch her she would certainly have been covered with mud—if she had not broken a bone or two!

At last the whole set of us were fairly packed into a saloon carriage, and now we were really "Westward bound!" The journey down to Westport was long and tedious, and nothing happened worth speaking about upon it: except just as Croagh Patrick came in sight, Master Ted began a melody of his own in a low, soft voice, which we at the other end of the carriage could not hear.

"Oh, look at the tip, the tip, the tip—oh! look at the tip o' Croagh Pa-trick!" he hummed, gently.

Maud and Willie let him go on for about five minutes, and then Maude exclaimed:

"Well done, Ted; bravo!—encore!"

But Ted was vexed that anyone had heard him, and so taking Maude's parasol he gave her a smart rap across the knuckles with it, for which rudeness his father reproved him.

At Westport there was a long car awaiting us, and then we started on our last stage for Fairlawn. Down the steep railway hill, past the Convent of Mercy, where one of my aunts had died, through the quaint old town, and then out into the open country. Auntie was very anxious to get a glimpse of Croagh Patrick and the three-hundred-and-sixty islands which beautify Westport Bay; but the evening mist was beginning to overshadow the land, and so we could only see as far as across a field or two. Little Ralph, the baby, was very tired and very hungry; so we stopped in Newport to get him some sponge rusks and a drink of milk. The owner of the shop happened to come out as our car stood before his door, and recognising us as the new-comers to Fairlawn, he treated us very courteously. He advised auntie to bring some provisions with her, "for," said he, "you will find nothing out there but eggs, and possibly a loaf of bread; your luggage, I fear, will not reach you until very late to-night." And so auntie took his advice, and there and then opened her account with Mr. Smith.

Ever since we had left home I had been dreading that we had to go down a rather steep hill just outside Newport: before, when I had been in the West, it used to be my bugbear, as we usually passed it in winter and at night; now, however, both the boys cried out together:

"And is this the famous hill, Mollie?"

"Yes," I answered, rather timidly.

"Well, if you aren't a milksop! Why, it's no hill at all!"

"Oh, you may say what you like," I said, resentfully, "but you wouldn't care to go *up* it with the ground frozen and the horse slipping at almost every step, and you in terror of being thrown down backwards every minute!"

Just then we met an outside car tearing along the road.

"Musha, an' where are ye goin' to, dhrivin' like that for dear life?" exclaimed our driver, a regular old Irish carman.

"Been to Fairlawn wi' a telegram," answered the other.

Auntie and Uncle Ralph looked at each other in surprise, and I don't know what made the latter ask:

"And do you know what it is about?"

"Yes, your honour; it's from Captain O'Hara to the steward beyant, telling him to let yez in." And with that comfortable information he left us.

All the rest of the way we children spent in wondering what this telegram could mean. "Such an idea," we agreed, "to be telling anyone to let us into our rights! What had Captain O'Hara to say to it at all? Wasn't it Uncle Ralph who had taken the place?" Maude herself joined in our speculations. At last we arrived there; and with a sudden jerk our old carman drove the machine into about the most original stable-yard *I* ever saw. It was simply a hill overgrown with grass, and with huge stones jutting out here and there to make the descent to the Lodge all the more difficult. At the top of this hill there was a row of dilapidated hovels, in which the coachman, a man-of-all-work, and his wife were supposed to live; together with a shed close by, which served as a stable to two wretched-looking horses.

There was a great congregation assembled to receive us; I think most of the inhabitants of the surrounding villages must have turned out for the occasion. One respectable man, however, came forward and helped auntie, and then Maude and me, to alight; and then Uncle Ralph asked about the telegram.

"I sent a telegram to Captain O'Hara this morning, sir," said the steward (for it was he) in a voice which sounded as though it came out of his shoes, it was so hollow and bass. "I sent him a telegram, saying I would admit nobody but him to the place, as Captain Maude mentioned no Mr. O'Connor in his despatch to me; but the telegram this afternoon from Captain O'Hara authorizes me to leave you enter."

This sounded a very cool speech, especially as Uncle Ralph had rented the place from Captain Maude. Maude's father had only gone with him during his interview with the owner in London.

Uncle Ralph said nothing to Sheehan, but asked the way to the house; and as they went slowly along—for auntie had sprained her knee —he explained how Captain Maude must have made a mistake, and taken HIM for Captain O'Hara, and Maude's father for Uncle Ralph; his right hand had been very much swollen with gout at Vichy, and so the Captain had written most of the letters about the shooting lodge, and that was how the mistake came about.

Meanwhile, we children had galloped down the hill at full speed, leaving auntie and Uncle

Ralph to follow as best they might. We set up a war-whoop when we sighted the house, Will, Ted, and I, for Maude was sensible, and therefore quieter. In we rushed to the Lodge, nearly knocking down Honor the housemaid, who was there to receive us with her best courtesy. Then we bounced into the drawingroom, the dining-room, then upstairs to inspect the bedrooms, and discovering a blazing turf fire in every room, we voted the people at the "back of God-speed" regular bricks: forgetting, however, that fires were necessary in a place which had been uninhabited so long. Then auntie and Uncle Ralph arrived, and Ted and I slipped away and out at the back door, "just to have a look at the place *out*side as well as *in*side," we said.

Down we sped, then, by the steep, narrow path, till we reached the beautiful shore of Lake Buckhough. The twilight was deepening fast, but still we could see enough to be sure that our new home was wonderfully wild and beautiful. Ted jumped on the little wooden landing-stage that ran far out into the water. It looked a very rickety affair to me: only an old rotten plank, held to the posts by rusty bits of iron.

"Ted, Ted," I cried, "get off that, sir, or you'll surely be in!"

"Can iron break, you silly?" he answered, coolly, beginning at the same time to dance and sing; but he danced just one step too many, and then I saw him in the water beneath! Fortunately it was low tide, and he was not wet above his ankles; however, his boots and stockings were quite damp; and where were we to get others, as the trunks had not yet arrived?

"Come, Ted," said I, "we'll go shares; you shall have my boots, and I'll go in my stocking-feet. Come along, off with these wet things!"

He was only a schoolboy, so he offered no resistance; and having had enough of the lake for this our first night, we retraced our steps to the Lodge, with our arms on each other's shoulders, brother and sister like.

"Listen, Ted," I said, presently, "isn't the babbling of that brook delightful? I should so like to take off my stockings and paddle a bit."

"Oh, come on, Mollie," said Ted; "we've had enough dowsing for one night. There's Will calling us; come on, do."

"Mary, Edward—Ma-ry, Ed-ward!" we heard called all over the place.

"Com-ing," I screamed, in a shrill treble.

"In the name of all that's good and holy, where

have you been, you two?" cried Willie, when he had found us. "Mother's been imagining you buried in the waters of the deep blue lake! Hallo, Moll, where did you get the light boots?—the luggage hasn't come yet, has it?"

"Oh, Will," I entreated, "for heaven's sake don't say anything! Ted tumbled into the lake and got his feet wet; so I gave him my boots, and I'm in my stocking-feet;—but sure you won't tell?"

But I could not hear his answer, as he had already turned into the diningroom, where the rest of the family were seated at supper. This last looked neither very appetising nor inviting. It was Friday, and therefore a fast day; so there was nothing but boiled eggs, bread, butter, and tea. But we were all very hungry after our long journey, and so we did justice to the only fare with which Fairlawn presented us.

"Come, Ralph, you're doing nothing," said auntie, during a pause in our children's prattle; "these children have already demolished two eggs a piece, and you've not got through your first."

"I can't manage with this scut of a spoon," said Uncle Ralph, disconsolately, holding up a doll's china spoon.

"Oh, Uncle Ralph, I'm so sorry," we all cried; "here take my spoon; take mine!"

There were only four German silver spoons in the place, and so after a great deal of fighting which should be most generous, Uncle Ralph took mine; but this sacrifice was not in reality an act of generosity on my part, for I had finished my supper before he made his complaint.

After we had finished the meal, auntie proposed that we should all retire without delay to Bedfordshire—a behest which Maude and I obeyed without murmuring. We two were to sleep in the room next the nursery; one of our windows overlooked my sweet little brook, and the other on the only garden of which the shooting lodge boasted. Neither of us slept very much that night: the change from our nice soft beds at home to these hard straw mattresses was indeed great; and I turned and twisted all night long, without getting any sleep, or at all events very little. The dawn arose bright and early next day, and awoke us with its first streaks: but there were no crimson flooded and golden glories of sunrise and sunset for *us:* because there were mountains to right of us, mountains to left of us, mountains behind us, which volleyed and thundered when storms came and shook them. Only in front of us there were no mountains, at least not for a long way off, and there Croagh Patrick, with his "head so tall and his sides so bare" bounded the view for us.

"Come, Maude," I cried, shaking her, "up with you, and let's go for a ramble and exploring expedition before breakfast: it'll be *so* jolly. I daresay the boys are out long ago!"

"What o'clock is it?" said Maude, rubbing her eyes.

"Just five. Come, don't be lazy;—see, I'm half-dressed already!"

Maude needed no second bidding; and in twenty minutes more the two of us were downstairs pounding at the boys' door.

"They *must* be out," I said at last, when no answer had come; "let's open the door and see."

But the door was locked: and with a farewell thump we were just leaving it, when a drowsy voice said: "Who's there?"

"Go to bed, says sleepy head," I called through the keyhole. "Here it is half-past five and a glorious morning, and you two boys snoring away there. Good-bye; we are going!"

"Oh, wait for me!" pleaded a voice I knew to be Ted's, as I heard him dashing the cold water in his sleepy eyes.

"All right; if you're out here in five minutes from this time we will wait. I am here, watch in hand; but the instant the needle touches the last second you're done for, and we depart!"

Then there was a great scuffling inside the room; and before the five minutes had run out, the boys appeared, not looking, however, as though they had attended to every item of their toilets.

"Now, where shall we go?" said Maude and I together.

"To the lake, of course," decided the boys; and so down to the lake we went. I think I never saw any scenery so lovely as that which broke upon us now. The deep blue waters of the lake, three miles long and one mile broad, from which rose all around the gentlest elevations, clothed with green meadows and waving cornlands; and then behind them again the great towering mountains, bare save for a few little patches of purple heather which grew here and there upon them, and the great boulders and rocks which jutted out to warn adventurers not to try and scale them in those places; and last of all, the deep, deep blue sky above the mountains again, with the sun stealing slowly over the shoulder of Buckhough! I could not help sitting down on the beach to admire the view, and I had just got into a comfortable position, with my hands clasped round my knees, when Ted called out impatiently:

"Oh, come along, Mollie; you're no good to go exploring with if you're going to sit mooning there!"

"I don't very well see how I could 'moon,' Ted," I replied, "when it's only just sunrise." However, I got up and followed the others round the shore to where a group of cattle were standing, some in the water and some drinking at its edge. Then we went back to the pier, and the boys insisted on getting into the boat. Maude and I tried to prevent them, but of no avail, and so thinking we might as well be "slaughtered for a sheep as a lamb," we went in also. However, the oars were nowhere to be found, and so we had to abandon our boating expedition. Then we skirted the lake in the opposite direction to the cattle, and went so far that we forgot the time, and when we looked at our watches we found it was twenty minutes to eight, and auntie had said the night before that breakfast was always to be at eight to a minute, and *I* had volunteered to be housekeeper, and here was I two miles and more from the house, and only twenty minutes to run them in. Then in a fit of contrition, away I sped at full gallop; but I was soon out of breath, and had to walk slowly, until the others caught up with me."

"Good gracious!" I cried; "it's just eleven minutes to eight; and look how far off the Lodge is: it looks like a little speck among the trees!"

We did our best, but that best was bad, to be in time; and it was twenty minutes past eight when the four of us ran into the house panting and tired with our long run.

"I had a little housekeeper once upon a time," said auntie, shaking her head as she poured out the tea, "but she ran away and left me, without even a minute's warning. I wonder shall I summon her at the next assizes?"

"O auntie," I said, penitentially, "I am so sorry; but really the morning was too lovely, and the place too tempting, and so we went for a ramble. You're not vexed, auntie, are you?—say you're not vexed with me; I promise never to do it again!"

"My own little woman," she said, lovingly,

stroking my hair, "it's a real pleasure to me when you are pleased. I did not bring you down here to be shut up in the house, but to get strong and well before you go back to your dear Mothers!"

"The luggage has come, mother," cried Ted, bursting into the room. "Hurrah! we can have something nice for breakfast. Come along, Mollie, and let's get out something!"

"Shall I, auntie?" I asked.

"Yes, dear; I think perhaps your uncle would like some ham; and tell Mrs. Fowler the first thing after breakfast to make some brown bread for him!"

"Good-morning, my pigeon," I said, as I saw Baby Ralph, the pet of the house, and my especial property, coming downstairs in his nurse's arms.

"Miss Mollie! Miss Mollie!" he screamed after me, "turn and div Waaf a kiss!"

Nothing loath, I obeyed; and then I went into the kitchen; and there arose before me a mountain of trunks, hampers, and wine-cases.

"For goodness' sake, Mrs. Fowler, which is the ham in?" I said.

Fortunately the cook knew where she had

stowed everything, and so we soon found what we were looking for.

After breakfast the boys went out shooting with Uncle Ralph and the two gamekeepers; and auntie, whose strained knee prevented her going about much, sat down in her own room to read and write letters. Then Maude and I set to work in earnest: she unpacked all the trunks, and I undertook to arrange the storeroom and pantry.

On Sunday only four of us were able to go to Mass, as the chapel was six miles away, and the old trap which belonged to Fairlawn could only hold Uncle Ralph, Will, Maude, and the nurse, besides Pat the coachman. Ted had a little croupy cough that morning, so auntie made him stay in bed; and then she went through some spiritual exercises with me until nearly twelve o'clock, when I took the baby up to the top of the hill to meet the churchgoers.

On Monday morning auntie was up at five o'clock, in spite of her bad knee, and she and Uncle Ralph drove into Westport to catch the morning train for home, where they intended to stay a week; so we children were left quite alone, with the three injunctions to the boys, not to shoot *grouse*, any other kind of game they could find they might bring down, though; not to go out on the lake without either Sheridan, the keeper, or Mick, his son : and not to drown themselves, or in any other way injure themselves! The house and Ralph were left in Maude's and my charge conjointly, and thus auntie left us. What a happy, happy week we spent down there all alone, in the wilds of beautiful Connemara! Nearly all day long the boys were out either shooting on the mountains or fishing in the lake; while Maude and I spent nearly all our time embroidering by the water's edge, or drifting slowly down its bosom to the other end. The following Tuesday we had a letter from auntie to say she was in Westport, and that I was to go in to meet her with the trap as she had brought Aunt Eliza, an old lady eighty-one years of age. I ran upstairs to get ready, and away to the stable on the hill to order the car; Pat was not long putting to; and soon we were spinning along as fast as the bad roads would let us, and the sleepy horses would go for us. Arrived in Westport we went up to the Convent of Mercy, where we stayed till two o'clock chatting with the dear good Mothers and Sisters, who had known and loved Aunt Theresa, and Sister Mary Augustine, a cousin of ours; and then we drove home, just as the hot afternoon sun was at its height. But we were amply repaid for our discomfort: for on the brow of the hill, midway between Newport and the Lodge, we had a glorious view of Clew Bay and its countless little islands. The sunlight was dancing on the sparkling water, looking like a very mirror for clearness, and the islets rose out of it, some dark and brown with heather, others fresh and green like their mother, the "Emerald Isle." It was only by dint of continual refreshment that we managed to land Aunt Eliza safely in the house; she was very, very old, you see, and aged people dislike moving from one place to another very much. But in a day or two she got accustomed to our life in the backwoods, and seemed to enjoy it immensely. She even said she "should be very sorry when those men (meaning Uncle Ralph, the Captain, and two or three more friends, who were coming down for the shooting) who were coming next week, would put an end to our gipsy-life."

On Thursday another Beaumont boy came to Fairlawn, Willie's great chum, and so there was one more to romp, and one more to add his share to the general uproar. But I must make haste and tell you of the last day *I* spent in the West. It was Tom's birthday (Willie's friend), and auntie first proposed to drive to Achill and the Kim Cliffs, but we all cried out: "No, no, a day on the lake and a scramble up the mountains!" and so we carried the day.

By cock-crow, almost, next morning, Maude and I were up, cutting chicken and ham, and packing a basket with good things for our dinner; and then, after a hasty breakfast, we all, except Aunt Eliza, Baby, and his nurse (who were left at home sorely against my will), got into the boat and were rowed across the lake by Sheridan and his son. The post-bag had just come in before we left, but nearly all its contents were for auntie; I got a letter or two from some of the Mothers in Paris, and Tom got some birthday packets; but Maude and the boys got nothing at all.

Then there was such a work to find a landing-place at the other side; the boys had to throw great stones into the water to make a pier, so as not to run the boat aground. We had no sooner touched land than they forsook us, and fled away up the hill, and left Maude and me to follow as best we might. But it was the tale of the hare and the tortoise, and we soon gained upon them. Half-way up the mountain I declared I could go no further, and so I turned and went down again. I knew I should have a great deal to go through this next week, which was to be my last at home, and whose happiness, I thought, could not possibly be compared to that awaiting me: but alas! how little could I foresee the future—instead of sunshine, all clouds and darkness and mistakes awaited me. Henceforth, it seemed my path lay through doubt and difficulty; and though I now know everything happened for the best, I then thought I had said good-bye forever to all earthly happiness or pleasure.

I had got to the bottom of the mountain now, but an immense bog lay between me and where auntie was sitting, writing letters: I crossed it bravely, not, however, without many a stumble and fall, and then I threw myself down beside her, utterly tired, and we began to talk about ourselves, and the boys, and everybody.

"They must be nearly here now, auntie," I said; "I'll go and get Sheridan to light the fire;" for we had brought potatoes, and a saucepan to boil them in, gipsy-fashion. The gamekeeper made a grand fire of some turf he found about the bog, and when the "Murphies," as the boys called them, were cooked, I could not resist eating one. But before I had finished, the young mountaineers made their appearance, and then we had dinner.

The boys were very fond of my lemonade; so I had filled some bottles with it to-day as a surprise for them. We had to eat, like Adam and Eve, for I, like a scatterbrain, had forgotten to put knives and forks in the hamper. I don't think Tom liked this proceeding very much; however, he had to put up with it. After dinner we had great fun washing the plates in the lake, for auntie made each of us, even the boys, take their share; and then as the sun had gone down behind Burrishoole, and it was getting cold, we prepared to go home.

Rowing back, Maude and I each took a little oar: I did it better than she; but, then, I had been used to row long ago, and I don't think Maude ever handled an oar in all her life; which, to be sure, was not *so very long!*

Directly we landed, the boys made us retire, as they wanted to bathe; and then Maude helped me to pack up a few things I had not time to do before.

That last evening was a sad one; poor Ted cried very much, he and I had always been such chums; and even Frank and Tom were very quiet. I alone of all the party was cheerful and I could not understand *why* they pitied me so much—perhaps they saw the "foreshadowing of coming events." I slept with auntie those last nights; and next morning she called me at four o'clock, as we had a long drive before us. Maude came with us into Westport;—poor Maude! she, too, cried a good deal at parting, and I—I shed not a tear: mine were all to come after!

Auntie stopped at Claremorris, and took me out to Knock, the place where Our Blessed Lady is said to have appeared. There was an immense crowd walking slowly round the chapel as we came in sight of it, and as we drew nearer we discovered that they were saying the Fifteen Mysteries of the Rosary. Their devotion was great and very impressive. We spent two hours there saying our prayers and buying little relics of the place, and then we drove back to Claremorris for the up train in the afternoon.

Ten minutes after that I caught my last glimpse of Croagh Patrick, and then tall Nephin faded gradually from my sight. There *were* tears in my eyes this time, at any rate, as I turned to auntie, and said: "Well, good-bye; a long, long good-bye to the West! I shall never, never see it again, and I thank God for it!"

"Yes, my own god-child, He will more than repay you for your sacrifice; He never allows Himself to be outdone in generosity!" said auntie, drawing my head on her shoulder. "He is always a God who *gives* more than He *takes!*"

Eighth Night.

A TEN MILES' GALLOP, AND WHAT CAME OF IT.

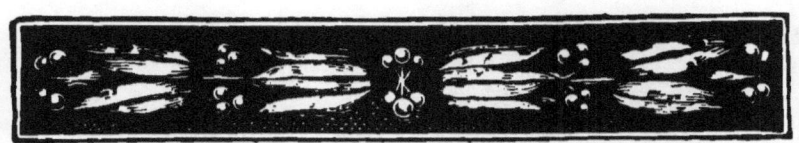

A Ten Miles' Gallop, and what came of it.

IT was a bright, cold morning in early November, many years ago, and little Alick Thompson came sliding down the bannisters of the old staircase in Blakesley Hall. He was thinking deeply within himself, and wondering and wondering, oh, so many things.

Anne Matthews, the laundry-maid, was scrubbing the tesselated pavement of the entrance-hall, and did not notice the little boy who came down so quietly.

Suddenly he said: "Anne Matthews, do you think papa will let me do what I want to?"

"My goodness! Master Alick, you nearly

frightened me out of my seven senses!" exclaimed the girl, looking up from her work.

"Your seven senses, Anne Matthews! What rubbish! To begin with, you've only got five. But that's not to the purpose; I want to know if you think papa will let me do what I want to?"

"Indeed, sir, I can't tell until I know what it is!"

"Oh, it's something delightful, and something awfully easy for him to let me do."

"What's the something that's so 'awfully easy and delightful?'" said a voice from behind, and looking up, he saw his father coming downstairs.

"Oh, papa, you heard me, did you?" said Alick, disappointedly.

"Yes; I could not help it; only tell me what it is you want."

"Oh, papa, how can I? I'm so afraid you won't let me!" said Alick, coaxingly.

"Well, let's hear what it's all about, and then I shall be able to tell whether I can let you," answered Mr. Thompson.

"Oh, papa, don't you remember! It's the Meet at Three Cross Hollow to-day!" said Alick, anxiously.

"The Meet!—oh, yes, of course. Well, if it's

only that you want to go to, I say 'certainly:' James can take you in the trap, as Isabel is going to follow the hounds to-day."

"Oh, papa, that's not all," whispered the little boy, clasping his hands; "I've often driven to a Meet with mamma and Isabel, but—but——"

"Oh, I understand now what you're feeling after, young sir," said his father, laughing; "nothing less than the run itself will suit you!"

"Oh, papa, will you, will you, please, please let me go?" pleaded Alick, gaining courage from Mr. Thompson's laughing mood. "James has been training me and Brenda to follow for the last six months; you needn't be an atom afraid. Oh, papa, please—please——"

"And what would your mother say to me if you were returned to her a bag of broken bones, eh?"

Alick was just going to say that he was sure she would not mind, his heart was so set on this run; but then he remembered how tenderly his dear mother loved him, and so he said: "Well, papa, if mamma says 'yes,' will you?"

"Yes, if mamma says you may, then I have no more to say."

"Hurrah, hurrah!" screamed Alick, as he

dashed upstairs two at a time, nearly knocking down his sister Isabel in his great speed, for he knew he could coax his mother into letting him have his heart's desire.

In about a quarter of an hour he appeared in the breakfast-room, holding Mrs. Thompson's hand, and looking very triumphant: it was quite evident that he had carried the day.

"Father," said Mrs. Thompson, addressing her husband, "we want you to grant us a favour."

"Well my dear, what is it?" he asked, knowing quite well all the time.

"It's the Meet at Three Cross Hollow this morning, and we should. *so* like to follow the hounds; but," added the lady, "if you think it wiser not, we will gladly do as you think best."

What a wise mother that was to teach her little son perfect obedience to his father in all things!

"Oh, that's for you to decide, my dear; if you don't mind the probability of his being brought home to you half dead, it's all right."

"I've no fear," whispered Mrs. Thompson, stroking the curly head. "Brenda is as safe and sure as she can possibly be, and he has looked forward to his first run so long and so eagerly. Then, father, it's settled; he may go?"

"Of course, since you wish it, dear: only James must keep close to him all day, and never leave him an instant. You had better run, Alick, and tell him to send round Brenda with the horses for Isabel and me!"

Alick needed no second bidding, and I verily believe James was as delighted as the child himself: he said he was sure that his darling little master would not only be "in at the finish," but he even went so far as to declare he would come off with the brush.

Three Cross Hollow presented a gay scene that November morning: the sun was shining brightly on the red coats of the gentlemen, and the blue sea shimmered and sparkled gloriously in the distance. Everybody was chatting with somebody, and everybody was surprised that Mrs. Thompson allowed so young a child as Alick to hunt. But these remarks did not damp Alick's pleasure; his father was a sportsman, and he had inherited his love of the field from him.

James, the groom, was very fond of his young pupil; and when the huntsman's horn blew, and the whip shouted, "Tally-ho! tally-ho! for'ard," Alick and Brenda were away before the others had collected themselves.

And now the real excitement began. To keep to the front was Alick's aim, and he succeeded admirably; while James never let more than half a field go between him and his charge. But if Master Alick thought he was not going to have any tosses during this, his first hunt, he was greatly mistaken.

They were crossing green sward, only divided into fields by narrow streamlets which were almost hidden by the grass. Suddenly they came to a wide one, and James, seeing it, shouted: "Don't take it, Master Alick, don't take it! The pony's legs are too short!"

But his warning came too late; Brenda had already drawn back apace for the jump; but instead of clearing it neatly as she intended to do, her foot slipped, and she and her little rider fell heavily into the stream. It was not deep; but the pony had thrown the child, and then fallen across his body, so that the little lad could scarcely breathe. To this day he remembers distinctly the thoughts that passed through his brain.

"What a mercy," he said to himself, "that the bottom of this stream is pebbly and not sandy! I wonder shall I be killed here! How glad I am I went to confession yesterday, as mamma told me! What will she say when I'm brought home to her all cold and dead! Oh, mother! mother!" And then he recollected how she had taught him always to say the Litany of the Holy Name in moments of danger, and so he began: "Lord, have mercy on us; Jesus Christ, have mercy on us!" And then he felt, as it were, a strong hand between his body and the pony's; and then he was tenderly lifted up by his faithful friend James. Then all poor James's Irish came out:

"Musha, me poor darlint, and are ye kilt intirely? *Wirra! wirra!* how was it I took ye this way, at all at all!" And he looked piteously at Alick.

"Why, James, I'm scarcely a bit the worse," answered the boy, "only for the ducking; come, let us mount, only I shan't get the brush to-day, as I hoped to!"

"Saving your presence, Master Alick," said James, "that same I can't allow. We must make for home now; you're not fit to follow any more!"

"Oh, James, please let me," said Alick; "really I'm not a bit hurt. See how well I can jump into the saddle;" and he tried to spring. But the weight of Brenda's body had been too much for his young strength, and he himself was obliged to give in to the groom, and be led home to the Hall again.

You can imagine Mrs. Thompson's fright when she saw her little boy again; and also how thankful she was that nothing worse had happened to her darling.

And so that is what came of the ten miles' gallop after the Blakesley hounds!

Katie's First Communion.

*"Et les Anges nous envient
Cet Aliment du Ciel."*

FRENCH HYMN.

YOU all remember Miss Swippie, don't you? Surely she and all her naughtiness cannot yet have faded from your memory, eh? Well, Miss Swippie had a cousin about four years older, who was, considering her advantages, quite as naughty: *her* name was *Katie* Hillyard, and she had been at school with the nuns nearly three years now; but, oh, me! did she not give them trouble!

One day the mistress-general, a dear mother whom God has since taken to be with Himself in heaven, called Katie, and told her that she was so naughty that she could not let her make her First Communion, as she had intended doing, on the 6th of May. Poor Katie cried very much when she heard this sad news; for although she was thoughtless and careless, she always loved our dear Lord very much, at least *she* thought she did; but *I* think that when one loves a person one shows it by trying to please them, don't they? Mother Carlton saw how sorry she was, and then told her if she would try—oh, ever so hard—to be good, she would think about it, and see if she could alter her decision. And from that hour nobody could believe their eyes, Katie became such a good child. The Mothers used to say to themselves, "Surely it is a changeling, for Katie Hillyard could not be so good!"

A short time after this, one of the mistresses, whom Katie loved very much, became dangerously ill, and the doctor said it would be a miracle if she ever came to the school again. Then Katie went to the chapel, and asked our dear Lord to make Mother Alice well again, and she promised Him to make all the acts of self-denial she possibly could for Him, if He would but grant her request.

Etta Wilson—Mother Wilson's niece—was Katie's great friend, and so she confided to her all her sorrow about Mother Alice.

"Won't you help me to make acts, Etta, too?"

she said, "and I'm sure that Jesus will hear us then."

Etta at once consented, and then they began to think what they could do that would please our Lord.

"Oh, I know," exclaimed Katie; "last week papa came to see us, and he left us lots of sweets. I've got a whole boxful of chocolates in my desk, and we'll go and leave it on the altar-steps and tell Him we are making Him a present of it!"

"But that would not quite do," said Etta, doubtfully; "the nuns would see it then, and ask what it was, and we don't want them to know, do we?"

"Of course not," agreed Katie. "Well, what could we do with it to make a sacrifice?"

"Let's throw it in the fire."

"Hurrah, capital! Stay, I'll go and fetch it, and we'll do it here now!"

While Katie was gone, Etta thought and thought, and at last she came to the conclusion that it would not be so great a self-denial to throw the box altogether into the flames as to drop each sweetie one by one into the fire. So then, when Katie returned, she heartily gave her consent, and they proceeded to consummate the sacrifice. It was a lovely French *bon-bon* box, with a pretty picture; but this, too, was to meet the fate of the goodies. First Etta took a chocolate, and dropped it into the fire, then Katie, then Etta, until there remained not one in the box; then this went like the rest, and then they went hand-in-hand and told Our Lord what they had done. And surely the ear that is ever open to the prayers of little children heard that prayer; for within a fortnight Mother Alice, in spite of the doctor's prophecy, was once more among her little ones.

By this time the First Communion Day was near at hand, and happily it was no longer a question whether Katie should be of the privileged number; for she had won her place, by great efforts and continual, over that little person "Self," who is *always* so hard to conquer.

Oh, how beautifully Mother Vernon, the Sacristan, arranged the chapel for that happy, thrice happy day. Early, very early, on the 6th of May was Katie awake, thinking that that very day she should taste, for the first time, the Bread on which the Angels feed.

At six o'clock the nun called the nine delighted children, and then they were dressed in their pure white uniforms and rose wreaths; each little one had a mother-of-pearl Rosary round her right wrist, and each wore on a white string round her neck a silver crucifix, on which was engraved her name and the date of her First Communion. By seven o'clock the whole school, numbering more than ninety children, was assembled in the chapel, all wearing white dresses; and then the nine children, whose most happy day had dawned, came in slowly, with Mother Alice at their head. The Cardinal himself came for this great occasion, and blessed and confirmed the little flock. Poor Katie! She said afterwards that she wondered how she could ever have been so naughty, when such a reward for being good was in store for her.

A great many friends came to see the happiness of the little ones, but Katie's parents lived too far away in Ireland to come all the way to England; but we may be quite sure the mother at home prayed much and earnestly for her darling, that the God whose seal had been that morning set on her forehead in Confirmation might bless and keep her, and accomplish only his most Holy Will in her.

And now, can you take a jump with me, and we shall land in the holidays—the midsummer vacation—when Katie is at home in Riversdale with her sisters, Mary, who is four years older, and Isabella, who is two years younger than herself.

The summer sun is shining blazingly in all his setting glory into the dear old breakfast-room, lighting up with his own bright fire rays the chandeliers, and playing fitfully among the dark curls of Katie, who is standing at the window, watching his last good-night.

The other children have long since left the tea-table, and run out hither and thither among the hayricks, or into the newly-cut corn-fields. The mother only sits silently at the table, watching the earnest and thoughtful countenance of her little girl. After a long pause Mrs. Hillyard says:

"Katie, darling, what are you thinking of?"

There is a little wait, and then the child answers, slowly:

"Oh, mamma, I'm thinking if it's so lovely down here on earth, what, oh! what must it be on the other side!"

A strange fear then takes possession of the mother's heart: she has never known Katie speak so seriously or look so earnestly before; but she chases her fears away, and calls the little one to her side, and begins to talk of the glories of that "other side;" the "land that is very far off, and where our eyes shall behold the King in His beauty."

The last day of the holidays has come—the happy, happy holidays with the father and mother, who do all they can to make the young lives of their children pass pleasantly. Katie has begged hard to be let stay at home for a year; she cannot exactly tell why, but she has a feeling which she cannot explain: and her father who loves her very, very much, thinks it only a fancy, and so says she must go back to school; it is for her good, or he would not send her.

It is, then, a cold day late in October; the school work has got into full swing once more, but Katie still longs for home as she never, never did before. She is very good, just as attentive to her lessons, as heedful of what the Mothers tell her, as she was last year—at least the latter part of it;—but there is a longing, yearning look in the great wistful gray eyes, and the never very rosy cheeks grow paler and paler day by day. It is Thursday, and consequently the children's confession-day. Many of them are sitting or kneeling, as the case may be, in the right-hand benches in the chapel, waiting their turns. Katie Hillyard is among the number, her hands folded and her eyes bent reverently. It will be some time before she can be heard, as she came among the last batch; but Mother Whittaker, who has charge of the confessions, notices her pale face and comes and tells her to go in next. And so Katie goes in, to what she little thinks is her last confession in that dear old chapel.

Next morning at Mass she feels so ill that, sorely against her will, she leaves the church. The dear mother who is Infirmarian thinks that a day in bed will set her up again, and so she sends her there. Poor little Katie! her head throbs and aches so that she forgets it is not right to get into bed with one's boots on, and so she does not take them off! Then for one long weary month she waits and listens—listens for the voice which she will soon hear, coming to call her across the river—waits for the Hand to hold hers while she passes through its cold, dark waters. She is patient and gentle through it all, through the worst of the hungry fever which is consuming her life; how patient, too, how tender are the Mothers in their watchful care of the child who formerly gave them so much pain, but who now seems about to be snatched away from them, just as the change for the better has come. But their watchword is *Fiat*—they know no other—and so they willingly, nay cheerfully, gave up the temple they have laboured to build for the King.

"Mother!" It is Katie who speaks in a low, feeble voice.

"Yes, my child, what can I do for you?"

"Please, Mother, may I have my First Communion dress near me?"

"Why, Katie?"

"Oh, Mother, don't you know?" she says, surprised.

"What, Katie?" asks Mother Reilly, as if to gain time, for *she* knows very well, only she is not sure whether the child knows that soon, very soon, she must say good-bye to earth; and so she says, "What, Katie?"

"Oh, Father Morgan told me something yesterday that made me so glad: only think, mother, I shall soon be at home in heaven, safe in the real Sacred Heart!"

Ah, yes, it is quite true; it is only a question of hours now; and the little one who won her crown so quickly yet so sharply, will be, as she says, safely laid near the real Sacred Heart.

Next morning Mary and Isabella ask their usual question of the mistress in their dormitory:

"How is Katie, Mother?"

And the Mother answers simply:

"Better."

And is she not quite right?—is not the darling little sister better, nay, quite well in the land where there is no more sickness and no more pain.

As she wished, she is dressed in her First Communion clothes, and the children come in one by one to say a little prayer at the death bedside of their companion.

Mr. Hillyard was telegraphed for the moment the doctor said there was no hope, and by the next mail he came; but—he was too late: the little spirit had taken flight, borne upwards on the wings of her guardian angel. Nobody had had the courage to tell Mary and Isabella until he arrived, and then, when they were told he was in the parlour, they both came running in, in the fulness of their joy at seeing their dear father.

Reverend Mother stood there, talking in a low voice to Mr. Hillyard, and turning she saw the children's surprised looks at his sad face. What could she say? Only the first words that came to her lips:

"Mary, my child, you must now comfort your poor father, for Katie is gone to heaven!"

Then, oh, then, the spring-tide of their tears was loosed, and they wept for the little sister who had left them so unexpectedly and so suddenly.

Dear little ones, for whom I am writing these

stories, perhaps you think that I talk to you too much about death, and tell you of too many people who died. But I don't think so: it is good to remember that we, too, shall one day have to do the same: it is good to remember, in the midst of this rushing, turmoiling life, that there is a Life which will never, never end; a Life, if we have earned it, to be passed with Him who is our Life; a Life whose joys "eye hath not seen, nor ear heard!" May the sweet Heart of Jesus grant that you and I may spend it with Him, praising Him endlessly and saying: Holy, holy, holy, Lord God Almighty; heaven and earth are full of the majesty of Thy glory.   Amen.

Ninth Night.

ANECDOTES.

A Legend.

THERE is a beautiful Italian legend about the birth of Our Lady, which I am sure you will like to hear. You all know what a legend is, don't you? A pious story, in which we are not bound to believe.

Well, then, this little legend tells that hundreds and hundreds of years ago, before even our Blessed Lord was born, that a poor little child died in the town of Nazareth, in Galilee. A beautiful shining angel came down to fetch it up to heaven, and in passing by a certain house with the child in his loving, tender arms, he saw the most lovely baby he had ever seen, lying in a cradle, with its mother watching beside it.

When at length he reached the gate of heaven

and had gone in with the little flower he had gathered on earth, he began telling his brother-angels what a beautiful child he had seen in passing by the house in Nazareth, and he declared that it was far lovelier than any angel in heaven; lovelier than anything that could possibly be imagined, except the Most Blessed Trinity. It was not very good of the angels; but they were not very pleased to hear that there was something or somebody lovelier than they were; so they began to wonder who it could be, and to dispute with the angel who had told them about the wonderful child.

Then God the Father hearing the noise, asked what was the matter, though of course He knew quite well beforehand. The angel who had just been down to earth came near to Him, and told Him, and so the Eternal Father sent the Angel Gabriel to bring this most lovely baby up to heaven that all the angels might see it, and judge for themselves.

St. Gabriel was not long fetching the little child, and soon re-appeared with his precious burden, which he gave into the arms of the Eternal Father; then He looked at God the Son, who smiled, and God the Holy Ghost, too, looked very pleased; for they all three knew that this most wondrously lovely babe was no other than the Blessed Virgin; and when the angels knew for certain who it was, they all agreed that she *was* more beautiful than any of them. Then the Angel Gabriel took the precious treasure in his arms and flew down to earth to place her in her cradle again. And you may guess how glad St. Anne, her mother, and St. Joachim, her father, were to get their little Mary back again, for *they* did not know where she had been.

* * * * *

I am now going to tell you about a lady who sang most beautifully, and who was very, very kind, especially to little children, whom she loved most dearly. Perhaps you may have heard somebody speak of her, for almost everyone knows that " Jenny Lind" sang beautifully.

Well, once she was in a very large town in Yorkshire, and she had promised to give a concert to help the large Infirmary of Hull, and so crowds and crowds of people came there to hear her, for all knew what a lovely voice she had.

Among the others were a lady and gentleman who were staying in the principal hotel with their little daughter, who was about eight years old. Lena (that was the little girl's name) knew that her father and mother had come to Hull expressly to hear Jenny Lind sing, and she hoped they would bring her also to the concert. So when the grand morning of the concert came, and Mr. and Mrs. Davis were seated at breakfast, Lena asked if she might go also. But her parents thought she was too young, and so refused to take her. This made Lena very sad, for she fully expected to go; and so she with difficulty kept from crying before her father and mother.

However, when they had done breakfast she left the room, and not being able to keep back the tears any longer, she sat down on the first window-seat she met on the stairs, and sobbed as if her heart would break. This was not a very wise thing to do, was it?—for after all, crying can never mend matters, can it?

Presently a lady who was coming down stairs saw poor Lena, and coming up to her she asked her what was the matter.

"I did so want to hear Jenny Lind sing," she said, between her sobs, "and mamma says I'm too young to go to a concert; and I'm so sorry I can't hear her; I do so love music!"

"Poor little woman," said the kind lady, stroking Lena's head, "don't you think that mamma would take you if you coaxed her very hard?"

"Oh, no; mamma never changes when once she says a thing," answered Lena, despairingly.

"Well, come with me, and we'll see if some goodies will make you forget your trouble;" and the lady turned back to her room, leading the sobbing child by the hand. The sweeties were very nice, but still they did not take away the sad look from Lena's face; so at last the lady said: "Shall *I* sing to you? will that do instead of Jenny Lind?"

"Oh, no," said Lena; "I only want to hear Jenny Lind; and I'm sure you can't sing as well as she; you don't look as if you could."

"Well, but won't you let me try and do my best," said the lady, amused at Lena's simple straightforwardness.

"Oh, you can if you like," said Lena, graciously, "only I know you won't be able to."

Then the lady opened the piano, and sitting down to it she began to sing the simple little song, "Coming thro' the rye."

The lady's voice was so clear and sweet, and the notes so rich and full, that Lena opened both her eyes and mouth in wonder to hear that marvellous voice; and when the lady had done, and was closing the piano, the child heaved a great sigh and said:

"That was very, very beautiful; but oh, you're *not* Jenny Lind!"

"Am I not?" said the lady, laughing. "Well, come up here to-night at half-past seven o'clock, and see if I shall not be dressed ready for the concert."

"Oh, yes, you may easily be that, but still you're not Jenny Lind!"

Just then a gentleman came into the room and began: "Jenny, my dear——"

"*Now* will you believe that I'm Jenny Lind?" said the lady.

"Oh, yes," cried Lena; "and thanks, hundreds of thousands of times, for singing to me: I must be off and tell mamma all about it." And away she ran to Mrs. Davis's room to tell of her wonderful adventure. It was very kind of Jenny Lind to do this for a poor little girl who wanted to hear her sing, was it not?

An Adventure on Lough Swilly.

PERHAPS you don't quite know where Lough Swilly is? Well, then, I will tell you. It is an inlet of the great Atlantic Ocean on the north-west coast of dear old Ireland. I need not tell you that it is a very lonely spot, for nearly all Donegal, the county in which it is situated, is that. Still there are a few gentlemen's houses scattered here and there, and the one with which we have to do is placed on the gentle slope which rises all around the lough. It belonged to a Mr. Armstrong, who had one child, a girl called Mina, and with her were staying the two daughters of Admiral Jones, who was in surveillance on the north coast.

It was a blazingly hot day; the sun shone unmercifully, and seemed to say, in all the independence of conscious strength: "I don't care; I *will* scorch you!" The first part of the morning had been hard for Miss Harman, the governess, for what with the heat, and what with the teasing little flies and midges, Fanny and Lillian Jones found it impossible to learn.

"Oh, Miss Harman!" exclaimed Fanny, in despair, "it's entirely too hot to study: we'll do extra work to-morrow, indeed we will, if you let us down to the lake now!"

"Yes, please, Miss Harman, do, do," chimed in Mina and Lillian together.

But Miss Harman did not require so much pressing; she was herself as eager as they were to breathe the little fresh air there was, and so she let them have their way. They were quite old enough to be left alone: for Mina was fifteen, Lillian thirteen, and Fanny eleven; therefore Miss Harman did not think it necessary to go with them to the lake. She did not fail, however, to give them many parting injunctions to be careful and steady, to all of which they duly swore fidelity.

Oh, what a grand thing liberty is! I don't mean that kind of liberty which is worse than imprisonment, and which permits us to give full swing to our evil passions; but I mean that joyous, full liberty which children enjoy in their hours of recreation, free from schoolroom restraint and silence!

The three children had tossed on untrimmed Zulu hats, and there they were running hand-in-hand, full tilt, to the water side, laughing and talking as only girls know how to do.

You will, perhaps, wonder that they *ran* on such a scorching day, but whenever did children bent on play and amusement *walk?* When, however, they had reached the lake they suffered for their speed, and then there was a great operation of wiping the perspiration from their brows. I have truly said that it was a hot day: the blue sky was cloudless, and the water without ripples, unmoved by the tiny breeze which tried but in vain to swell it.

"Oh! there's the boat!" cried Fanny; "let's get in and have a row!"

"Perhaps it would not be safe to go alone," suggested Mina, timidly. "You know there's the current in the middle of the Lough, and we might be capsized before we knew where we were!"

"Oh, rubbish!" said Fanny. "Who wants to go near the current? Why, we'll keep quite close to the shore, of course."

"All right, then; come along."

They were no sooner seated in the boat than they found they had no oars; so Fanny offered to run and fetch them from the boat-house, about ten minutes' walk off.

"Stay, Fanny," said Mina; "you cannot carry those great oars all alone. Let me come with you; wait for me!"

"Make haste, then; sharp's the word. Lily, you'll wait there, won't you? and mind nobody takes my place while I'm away," she added, laughing at such an improbable possibility.

"All serene: only do you both make haste back; it's dull sitting here alone." And saying this, Miss Lillian fell into a reverie, gazing with wide open eyes into the shallow depths beneath. Of what she was thinking I cannot tell; only whatever it was it must have engrossed her so much as to make her forget that she was on the water, and not only on the water, but on Lough Swilly, which is noted for the rapidity of its currents.

Mina and Fanny were not long away: still they were long enough for Lillian to get into danger during their absence; and when they returned with the oars they found that she had drifted out about what seemed to them an arm's length. However, they soon found it was much worse than that when they tried to haul in the boat. At each fresh attempt to grasp a rowlock she went further and further away from the shore. Then Fanny, who was a brave child, and who loved her sister very much, took off her shoes and stockings, and waded into the water, ankle-deep, knee-deep, but no further could she go, and still the boat was out of her reach.

"Oh, I know!" she exclaimed, paddling out of the lake, "here, Lillie, catch hold of this oar and we'll soon tug you in."

In vain; the more efforts Lillian made, the further the boat receded from the land.

In despair Fanny ran hither and thither; each moment Lillian's figure grew smaller and smaller; now she was nearing the dreadful current, that would hurl her in less than ten minutes into the wide Atlantic. Mina sat down on the shore, and began to cry; but what good did crying ever do to mend matters? Fanny, on the contrary, started off in her bare feet for help, away, away across the stubble-fields, where on another occasion the short stump of the newly-cut corn would have pricked her unendurably. But now she felt them not—her darling Lillian was in danger, and on she sped till she came to a group of reapers.

"Oh, come!" she cried, "come to the lough; my sister has drifted out in a boat, and we cannot reach her; come, oh, please come, and help us!"

They were poor Irishmen, who never yet saw

any body in distress but they did their little utmost to help them out of it. So they threw down their reaping-hooks, and followed Fanny to the water-side.

"She's all right, Miss," said one of the men, reassuringly to the poor little sister, whose face wore such a piteous expression of anxiety.

Lillian and her barque seemed but a little speck on the lake now, they were so far out. But Andy knew that she could not be engulfed in the current, for his sharp eyes could see that with a bit of broken oar she was sculling, and that kept her away from it.

By this time the men had got out another boat, and were already rowing towards the middle of the lough. Poor Fanny, her hands were clasped tightly, and her eyes strained to make sure the men had reached Lillian. Then she saw them lift her into their boat, and that was all she cared to see; so she breathed a sigh of intense relief, and sat down on the shore to wait.

After she had quite done kissing the sister, whom she thought she should never see again, she whispered that they ought to do something for the poor men who had come so willingly to the rescue.

"When papa comes next time," she said, "we'll tell him all about it, and I know he'll reward them."

"Oh, Miss!" said one of the poor men, "don't go for to be thinking of rewards; we don't want any—it's enough, and a pleasure, too, to see ye safe and sound on dry land again."

But Lillian and Fanny insisted; and when Admiral Jones came next time to see his little daughters, he heard the whole history; and do you think that any papa, who loved his children like Admiral Jones did, would leave unrewarded anyone who had saved one of those little ones from a terrible death. Indeed, no; those who cared for a sailor's life he employed on one of the ships under his command; and for the others he did something equally generous and grateful.

Barcelona.

WHAT! another story! Why we've only two minutes left, and you know we've got to go to the chapel to-night and offer our rose-wreath to the Blessed Virgin. Well, then, just one more little one. About what shall it be? Oh, I know. We've heard a great deal about England and Ireland. Let us have something now about Spain. I'll tell you what I know of Barcelona, a city in which I awoke one fine morning long ago. I wonder if you think of it, not having seen it, as I thought before I went there? I pictured to myself a small town with long, low houses, and wide, sun-scorched streets, with the blue Mediterranean sparkling and rippling to the east.

Not at all! it is not one bit like this. But a great crowded city, with narrow streets and numerous, in which, with the help of a sweeping-brush, you could shake hands across the way. The houses, instead of being long and low, as I expected, are very, very high, sometimes of six and seven storeys; and according to the number of flats or storeys so many families inhabit a house. A *ciel-ouvert*, as they say in France—I don't exactly know what they call it in England—gives light to the back apartments of all these flats, so that the rooms of the two lower ones, that is, the first and second flat, are very dark.

The streets of Barcelona are crowded; one can scarcely imagine where the people come from; for in what we call the back streets in England, it seems to me, some of the best families live. Then the beggars! I am sure the persons who say there are more beggars in Naples than anywhere else cannot have visited Barcelona. One is literally besieged with them: and if one were to give alms to everyone who asks them in *one* morning, one would certainly return home a beggar one's self. And there are so many—oh, such numbers of poor unfortunates that are deformed!—some who have their feet turned upwards, and so cannot walk; some who are blind, and therefore cannot work; and some again who have been born with no hands. And among these last, I must tell you of one whom I admired and respected, oh! ever so much. Her arms ended in stumps instead of hands, just about where the elbows ought to have been; but will you believe it, she worked for her living, and worked beautifully too! She sat by the wayside in a crowded thoroughfare, embroidering handkerchiefs all day long: before her was placed a little tin plate into which if you dropped an alms, she would take a paper and pencil and write your name. And as I passed her, I used to say to myself: "That poor woman deserves to be helped, for she tries to help herself."

The Rambla is a fine broad street, about a mile long. There are footpaths on each side, and then down the middle a very broad one, while the cars and cabs run between the narrow footpaths and this broad one. It is a pretty sight, in the early morning, to see the "Flower Market," which is held there. And such flowers! Imagine roses in March! Camelias, too, and real orange-blossoms! The women who own these stalls make such charming bouquets! Often and often have I longed to be able to transplant one of them to the High Altar in the dear old chapel so far away in England.

Then there is the Paseo de Gracia (Pass of Grace), which is much wider than the Rambla, and in which there are few, if any, shops. It is a pleasant place to sit in, under the shady olive-trees. And that reminds me, you would like very much to see oranges growing, should you not?

Well, they grow in abundance in Barcelona: and there are orange-groves without number. The Park is quite an affair of yesterday; still it is a very fine one; and there are many nice things in process of formation, such as cascades, miniature lakes, islands, &c.

As for the Mediterranean, one does not see it at all unless one goes quite to the end of the Rambla: and then it is only to meet wharves and quays, so that one does not get much of the "blue Mediterranean" at Barcelona.

You will like to know that there is a Convent of the Sacred Heart at Sarria, a little village not far from here; but as I have not been there yet, I cannot tell you what it is like. However, we may be quite sure the Mothers are the same there as everywhere, and as the only letter of introduction I have is my Child of Mary's medal, I don't much fear for the reception I shall have.

And now we come to the churches: and I am so sorry to have to tell you that I was disappointed, oh, so very disappointed with them! It is not that they are dark, no, for that seems to be the test of their antiquity; it is not that there are few chairs and no *prie-Dieus* in them; but it is the disrespect—it may be only seeming—of the congregation. Dogs are allowed to run about during

Mass; baskets of merchandise are brought into the churches—not certainly to be sold there—and most of the people have a disgusting habit of expectorating on the floor on which others are likely to kneel. Then the acolytes—during one Mass I've seen them change four times—and the way they fidget and answer the responses is very disrespectful to my mind. One of them usually goes round with the alms-box, and as he passes each altar has something to say which makes the server laugh and nod his head; another is seen trying to win a race with someone else into the sacristy; while a third flies thence with a black bottle, which contains, I suppose, altar wine. The cathedral here is, I believe, one of the finest in Spain; and it contains a miraculous crucifix which once gained a victory for the Spaniards over the Turks. Santa Maria del Mar, (Our Lady Star of the Sea) is another noted church, in which the statue of the Blessed Virgin is wonderfully lifelike. I do not say what I have complainingly of the churches in Spain, only that if you should come out here, you may not expect great things, and then be disappointed as I was.

* . * . * . * . * .

"And now there are only five minutes left; we must make haste to the chapel. Come along; your hats will do; there's not time to fetch your veils."

So then Helen, and Veronica, and I went into the church, where the shadows had long since deepened into darkness, and where there were but two nuns praying before the Blessed Sacrament.

Softly then we stole up to Our Lady's altar, and kneeling by the rails, I began to pray to myself.

"Why don't you say something?" said Veronica, presently; "why don't you tell the Blessed Virgin why we've come?"

"I will, dear," I said; and then I began this little prayer:

"Most dear and holy Mother, we Thy three children have tried to keep this Novena in a way we thought would please Thee, and so we have brought this little rose-wreath, and now humbly lay it at Thy feet, that Thou mayest bless it: and if it be Thy will that others besides ourselves should see it, we ask Thee to make it a blessing to them. Amen."

There was silence then in the great chapel, till the school-bell ringing warned us that we had nearly outstayed our time; and so leaving my two little chargelings at the door of the study-hall, I went back to the chapel to offer a sacrifice which has cost me many a tear and many a heartache. But it is God's will, and He knows always what is best for us: and feeling sure of this, as I do, I try to say peacefully and contentedly: "*Fiat voluntas tua sicut in cælo et in terrá.*"

And now, dear little ones, good-bye: *perhaps*, one day, we shall meet again; till then—if it ever comes—a long, a loving good-bye, and may the time from now till then be linked together by sweet thoughts of Her by whose inspiration and help these little stories have been written.

www.ingramcontent.com/pod-product-compliance
Lightning Source LLC
Chambersburg PA
CBHW031748230426
43669CB00007B/532